COPYWRITING IS...

30-or-so thoughts on *thinking* like a copywriter

ANDREW BOULTON

©

A *...Gasp!* **BOOK**
GASP FOUR LTD.
GREAT BRITAIN
Gasp.Agency

First published in 2021

For G and for P. *Always.*

"Andrew writes a love letter to copywriting. Not a how-to, but a how and why we write. For copywriters, it puts our sometimes inexplicable thoughts and behaviours around writing into wonderful words. For non-copywriters, it's a beautiful account of the parts of the process you don't see or understand. This is a book I'll read again and again."

– Vikki Ross, Copy Chief

/

"Packed to the gunwales with witty observations, valuable insights and timeless advice, Copywriting is... is a warts 'n' all interrogation into the different lives, minds and worlds of copywriters today. Perfect for junior writers and experienced wordsmiths alike, it's an inspiring, entertaining and addictive read."

– Gyles Lingwood, Author of Read Me

"Copywriting is as troublesome a word as it is a profession. It is, as you'll discover in Andrew's excellent book, a great many things. But it is also not a thing. It is a contradiction, a shared illusion. In truth, there are just different combinations of words and sentences. Some persuade you to feel something, some don't. What makes Andrew's book so enjoyable is that the words and sentences he combines to describe our shared illusion are so effective, they might just persuade you it's real."

– Glenn Fisher, Author of The Art of the Click

/

"If you love losing yourself in long copy, dip in!"

– Jane Evans, Creative, Activist & Keynote Speaker

"What to write about a book on copywriting? I read it (in one sitting). My mind wandered (a good thing according to the author). I learned two new words (eremitic and sesquipedalian). I searched up two of the sources (and plan to go back to the many useful-sounding ones). I think you should read this book (at least once a year, for the rest of your life)."

– Diane Young, Co-founder & CEO of The Drum

/

"I counted three unintentional rhymes in the last two pages. You are not Tupac. You are, however, a creative oddball which is why I like you. And why I love this book."

– Giles Edwards, Creative Director & Founder of ...*Gasp!*

"Copywriting is... wonderfully enigmatic, if this book is any indication. By drawing attention to the more intangible elements of our craft – with references ranging from Philip Larkin to Lethal Weapon – Andrew has put together a treatise quite unlike anything else out there. And perhaps unsurprisingly, it comes packaged in an effortlessly eloquent turn of phrase. I wish I'd written it."

– Ryan Wallman, Creative Director, Head of Copy & Author of Delusions of Brandeur

/

"The book I wish I'd read when I was starting out as a copywriter, why is it so late?."

– Sue Higgs, Group Creative Director

Acknowledgments.

In an ideal world, I would have woken up one morning from a *benzedrine haze* to discover I'd typed out an entire book in the space of a lost and frenzied weekend.

Sadly, that never happened and I was compelled to depend on my own appalling sense of concentration and discipline to get the job done. Which was gross.

But while my lazy and haphazard approach to real work hardly merits a 'thank you' on these pages, there are plenty of people around me who absolutely do. In no particular order...

Giles Edwards and the utterly wonderful team at Gasp!. We wasted most of our editorial meetings talking about Spurs, Alan Partridge and how he could possibly be a successful podcast host with such an irritating voice. But he has been the finest publisher, and pal, I could have hoped for on this journey.

Gyles Lingwood for the hours (genuinely, hours) spent helping me to not be such an idiot about the publishing world – and, more importantly, being my first real cheerleader in the pursuit of this project.

Captain Dave Pettitt and the whole University of Lincoln Creative Advertising team, past and present, for introducing me to a deeply rewarding life of helping young creatives discover a love of copywriting.

Reluctantly, the outstanding students I've met and taught on that same course, who are already soaring past me on their way to remarkable creative careers. This dedication is to help you remember my name when your lives are filled with fame and glory.

Dr Ben for doing what he's been doing since we were 11 – making me a better writer and not-quite getting me to understand how grammar works.

Cameron Clarke, and the tremendous team at The Drum, for giving me such a prestigious platform for my copywriting ramblings, for so many years – especially as so many of those ramblings have now Frankensteined their way into this book.

A copywriting community – both real and cyber – who do so much to make our job the most welcoming, generous, positive and supportive in the creative world.

My family, my beautiful wife, my bonkers daughter, my chubby cat, my ma and pa. My very much missed nanna and gramps for whom, ironically, I do not have enough words.

There are many, many other people I need to thank – and shall – but I've just finished writing a book and if I type one more word I will literally die.

This book is *not*...

Because it would be enormously undignified for a book on creative advertising to be guilty of false advertising, I'd better explain what it is you may *(or may not)* be about to read.

Or rather, I will be clear about what this book will not do.

It won't for example, walk you through some individual copywriting techniques and methods.

Nor will it show you specific examples of real-life ads and concepts to illustrate how these techniques are used.

The reason is quite simple. Writing such a book is far harder to do and I am far lazier than the sort of person who is able to write one.

More importantly, such books already exist and there are a handful of them I am entirely sure I would not be able to improve on.

Though it pains me greatly to say it, because I know one of the authors personally, Read Me by Gyles Lingwood (ugh) and Roger Horberry is as close to an indispensable copywriting manual as you are likely to find. All I ask is that you refrain from buying a full price copy as Gyles is unbearable enough without the royalty cheques.

Another excellent guide to specific copywriting methodology – and how it should be employed – is Mark Shaw's book, Copywriting. You should also take a look at Glenn Fisher's Art of the Click (for a more direct response copy focus) and anything Steve Harrison has ever written, even shopping lists or rude graffiti on a toilet door. A Vikki Ross book on copywriting will hopefully appear at some point, and you should be prepared to lose a prominent finger to get a copy.

Instead, what you have in your hands (or ears – ahoy there, audiobookers, never let anyone tell you this isn't proper reading) is a book containing some of my thoughts, feelings, fears, failures, frustrations and half-baked solutions from a life in copywriting, and the teaching of copywriting.

It is a book to be read in whichever way the pages fall.

At times it invites you to be thuggish and reckless and entirely carefree as you write. In other places it will make the case for treading lightly on the page. Neither argument is less worthwhile than its neighbour – it's your job to find yourself, your writing self, in the crowd.

A final word before you embark on the book (or quietly re-shelve it).

Books like this are a moment in creative time. They are how the creative world has appeared to one person, standing on one hilltop gazing out at one slice of the landscape.

Creativity changes and creativity does not exist in the same way for everybody.

Graham Greene wrote in an essay, called The Explorer, that 'the imagination has its own geography, which alters with the centuries'.

The imagination required in a profession like copywriting alters faster than that and yet, in many ways, it does not alter at all.

What I am saying, and it will sound preposterous, is do not let this book – or any book of a similar kind – become your creative bible.

Challenge what is said. Disagree, or at the very least think carefully about why you do agree. Treat this as nothing more significant than a handily placed stool that allows you to scale the walls of your own creative identity.

And, more than anything else, buy it at full price. Ideally twice.

Copywriting is

QUIET

(Or, the creative science of silence)

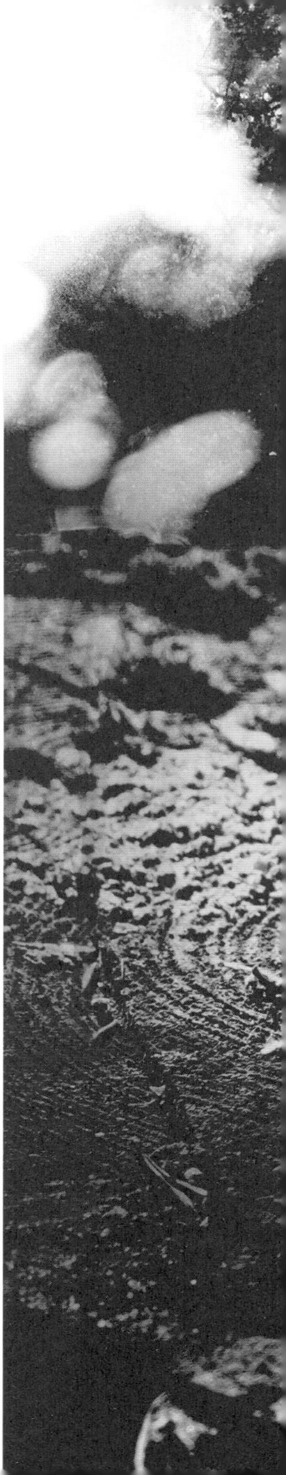

The *strangest* sound I ever heard in a creative studio – amongst a symphony of strange sounds – was the word 'mushroom' shrieked at the pitch usually reserved for announcing incoming mortar fire.

For context, it was because a designer had carelessly let slip to colleagues that she was both afraid of, and severely allergic to, mushrooms. Her desk, predictably, had been instantly stroganoffed with around 40 of the brutes.

Jostling for top spot in the hit parade of odd noises are a variety of cackles, wolf howls, clangs, crumples and even, once, the sound of a large cake being hit with a cricket bat – a sort of airless 'whoomp' if you're interested.

Compiling such an audio compilation – aside from making me consider the market for a 'NOW! That's What I Call Agency Chaos' cassette – made me ponder the environment we've created for ourselves.

Under the banners of 'collaboration' and 'creative energy' the studio has adopted the sort of sound ecosystem you would find in the canopy of a Brazilian jungle, or a Walkabout bar.

In many ways, there is nothing particularly wrong with such an atmosphere. The vast majority of people working in a creative agency are doing so precisely because the peace and uniformity of a 'regular' office makes them sweat.

But while the clatter of creativity is good for our wayward souls, it may not be as useful for our minds.

Now, my scientific knowledge extends no further than being able to identify, if not actually use, a pipette. However, I'm incredibly interested in the scruffy, hectic nature of what we do and the human chemistry behind what allows us to do it.

In particular, I'm fascinated by the conditions that govern the most intangible part of our work: the creative state.

There is (he said, with no great authority) a neurological state known as the default mode network. In slightly simpler terms, this is the state of self-generated cognition. In actually simpler terms, it is allowing your mind to wander.

The correlation between this state and creative activity has been well established, demonstrating the power of unconscious, or at least less actively controlled, thought to produce ideas.

It is, in a way, an invitation to idle – redefining what a productive working state looks like for a creative. I'm sorry, madam, but I shan't get out of this hammock – can't you see I'm default moding?

Stillness, of course, is not the same thing as laziness and if you use this knowledge as an excuse to nap or finesse your floundering fantasy football team you are perverting the science – and your fantasy football team will, invariably, remain woeful.

But, to enter this hallowed state of creative inspiration, we need to manufacture the right conditions. Allowing your mind to truly wander is easier to achieve in a quiet place than it is in a room filled with people arguing loudly about how to treat potentially fatal mushroom poisoning.

Stillness, quiet and calm are the triggers for the default mode activity that spawns your greatest ideas. Noise, chaos and, worst of all, a relentless, flapping 'busy-ness' suppresses it.

Now I'm well aware that not every creative enjoys quiet time. Working in isolation can be unsettling, even rather intimidating if you feel cut off from the challenge, support and filter of the creative pack.

But, allowing some time every day to let your mind quietly steer you somewhere new will make you a better creative and a better collaborator. Some agencies are even experimenting with designated quiet time, where the only focus is unfocused thought. No emails, no meetings, no chat.

So next time your studio erupts with the sound of a hundred monkeys in a bowling alley, seek out your quiet place and listen to nothing but the noise of your brain getting to work.

QUIET

Copywriting is

WANDERING

(Or, why desks can make your copywriting drab)

Some jobs are *fixed* to a certain environment. Pilots can only actually pilot if they are in a cockpit. Otherwise they're little more than an overdressed airport accoutrement, no more distinct in that setting than an uncomfortable plastic bench or the faint 'poof' of a suspicious duffle bag being blown-up by security.

Copywriting, on the other hand, is not tethered to a particular point. Except, of course, when it is. Which, of course, is a lot.

Survey the copywriters in your immediate circle and I'd be surprised if all of them did not spend most of their creative time in the same spot, working with the same apparatus, trying to scrape inspiration from the same surroundings.

In How to be a Graphic Designer Without Losing Your Soul, Adrian Shaughnessy says 'Our focus has narrowed. We rarely look at our work from a distance. We rarely look at it from different angles. We often work in miniature. We avoid anything that can't be done on the computer. The screen dictates our relationship to our work – it dictates how our work looks.'

Most copywriters are, willingly or unknowingly, drawn to confinement, soothed by the familiar. We are wild animals flinging ourselves in front of a zookeeper, eagerly volunteering to abbreviate our own territory.

On the one hand, it's understandable. Familiarity, comfort and the reassuring sovereignty of a habitual space all add up to a controlled and consistent place to work.

But, in our line of work, controlled and consistent can provoke an unusual sort of chaos. At the very least it breeds a stale sort of fluency that gradually erodes the need for imagination.

Also, how we choose the places we work is often more about conformity than suitability. We work at our desk because it is there and it is ours, not because it is necessarily the most effective environment for creative thought.

Consider this observation from Kenneth Roberts in his book, I Want to Write: 'Most spots, houses and rooms, no matter how sequestered, how uninviting to other activities they may appear, await only the presence of a would-be writer to develop habits, quirks or sounds discouraging to, or destructive of, unbroken thought and the uninterrupted concentration needed for sustained work'. Just as Roberts describes, your own habitual workspace could be unsuitable and restrictive in any number of ways – if you only looked for them.

W A N D E R

Rather than being the place we are most likely to write, the desk becomes the place where it is easiest not to. Often, without realising, we create the perfect growing conditions for distraction. The desk becomes the place where we stall and divert, where the work is unable to pin us down. And, as Tennessee Williams once wrote, 'the right condition for him [the writer] is that in which his work is not only convenient but unavoidable'.

It's also worth remembering we are, after all, not authors or poets with a distinct voice to refine and maintain. In their case, writing in the same way, at the same time, in the same setting may be essential to preserving the 'self' in their work.

But as copywriters, allowing a distinctly personal terroir to permeate what we write is the opposite of our basic function.

In other, less French, words there is a danger that writing in the same environment, and through the same behaviours, will only allow you to write in a style determined by the rigidity of your method.

In The Creative Brain, Nancy C Andreasen observes that a wandering mind 'leads to heightened perceptions, greater sensitivity to external stimuli and increased intensity of experience.' Now, unless that particular state would somehow get in the way of your best ideas, shouldn't we all be encouraging our minds to wander? And what better example to set for our brain than to allow our legs to lead the way?

Whether we recognise it or not, the conditions in which we write will inevitably seep into our process and therefore our output. It sounds simplistic to say that if we always write where we've always written, then we'll always say what we've always said. But there is a valid theory that, without adaptation, challenges and a shift in perspective, copywriting becomes more about easy answers than effective ones.

Essentially, the only signature a copywriter should leave behind is their invisibility (as Iris Murdoch says 'bad writing is almost always full of the fumes of personality'). Our purpose is to absorb, and be absorbed in turn, by the uniqueness of the brief, the problem, the voice and the audience. That leaves no room for an approach propped up by convention or throttled by routine.

For unknowable reasons, copywriting is one of those strange self-dogmatising professions – creating a perverted belief system in which stimulation is unnecessary and stagnation is allowed to go unseen.

And then, before we realise it, we're just sad pilots without a plane, wandering pointlessly through Duty Free, gazing wistfully at the big Toblerones.

Copywriting is

ABSORBING

(Or, living with a copy shadow)

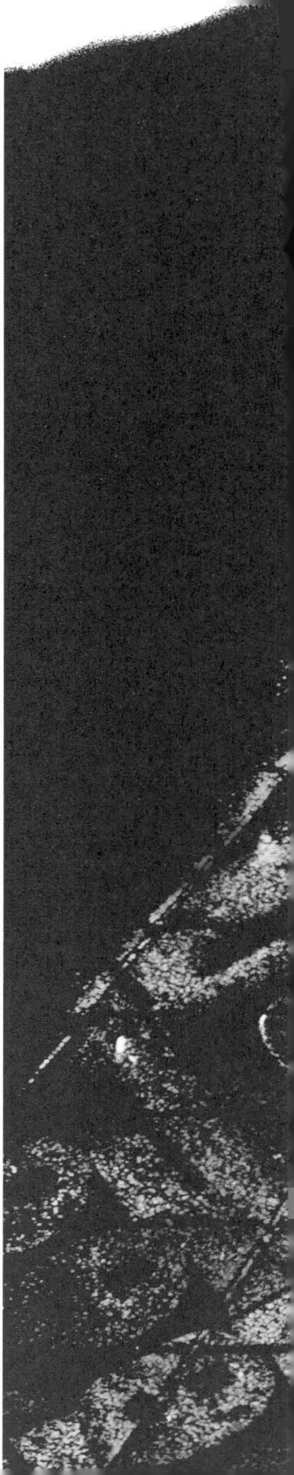

In Sarah Bakewell's excellent book on the creative life, *How To Live*, she talks about the great French author Montaigne – and his *shadow*.

Bakewell writes 'as Montaigne the man went about his daily life on the estate, Montaigne the writer walked behind him, spying and taking notes'. In other words, there must be two halves to every creative existence – the one that experiences the inspiring nature of their surroundings, and the one that makes sure neither of them forgets it.

In the previous chapter, we pondered the dangers of only ever working in one place. The counter-danger of working away from it (who knew copywriting was so fraught with peril?) is that great ideas can come and go before we have a chance to stun them with a heavy book and trap them in a jar.

No matter what your timesheet tells you, there is no such thing as downtime in copywriting. Just because you've finally managed to get out of the office, or away from a niggling brief, doesn't mean the work has stopped, or is indeed capable of stopping.

The writer who wakes in the middle of the night with a wonderful solution, but forgets it by morning, is a rampant cliché in any wordy profession. But it's also entirely true.

The antidote is mercifully simple. You may have no control over the thoughts you have or the convenience of when and where they arrive. But you are in complete control of your ability to record every idea, regardless of how deserving it proves to be of record.

This isn't a terribly original thing to be telling copywriters, but it is an important one. Many people have, more eloquently than me, urged anyone who writes to carry a notebook on them at all times (or a phone with a notes feature, if you're too young to have seen Con Air in the cinema).

My favourite of all these entreaties is from Michael Baldwin who, in his book The Way To Write Short Stories, expresses it like this:

'Anyone finding themselves swimming naked a mile offshore when the words come should scratch them immediately on a companion's back or bite them into the dorsal fin of a great white shark'. He finishes his instruction with the words 'nothing ever lasts in the head' and that is dangerously close to being the best piece of advice I can offer you.

Of course, simply being a diligent recorder of your ideas isn't enough to make you an exceptional copywriter. Much of what you write down, however interesting or original it may seem at the time, will either be no good for the problem you need to solve, or simply no good.

However, the habit of trapping your every observation at least gives you possession of your own ideas. It gives you a window into the strange and unpredictable workings of your creative brain – and even if you only use one in a hundred ideas you capture, it can only be a good thing to know a little more about what seizes your brain's attention and what does not.

The work your creative shadow puts in is less than half the job. Even with a new and valuable thought, the real-life part of you must be able to transform it into something clear and purposeful. But if you had to do that part of the job, as well as make up for your shadow's slackness and inattention, you will spend too much of your time trying to remember the thought you had that may, or may not, have been the answer to everything.

Copywriting is

COLLABORATION

(Or, find your Clemmit)

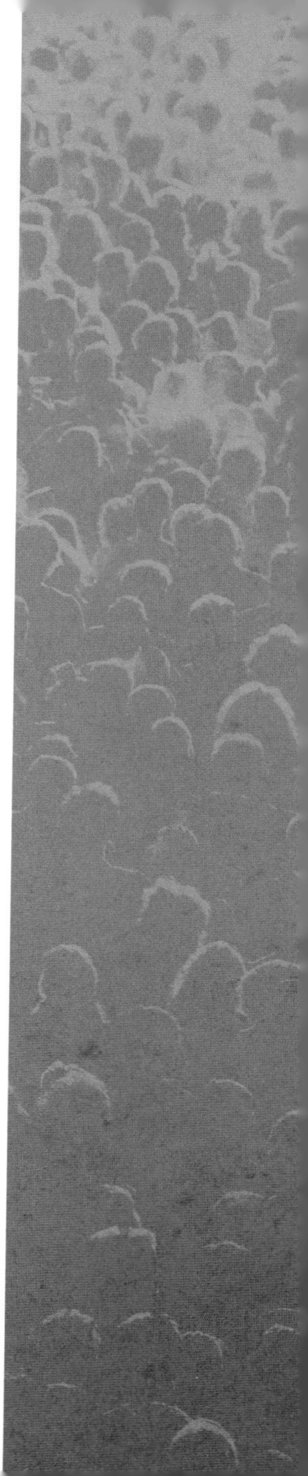

If Lethal Weapon had been a film about a lone detective, nearing retirement, quietly grumbling alone in his squad car that he's *'too old for this shit'* – despite finding himself in very little actual shit – it would have been a far shorter, far less interesting movie. You might even find yourself complaining there was nothing lethal, or indeed weaponised, about what you'd just seen.

Buddy cop action movies are, if only in this way, similar to copywriting.

Now, I know that many copywriters would sooner socialise with a pouch of Scrabble tiles than spend too much time in the company of, urgh, people.

But however appealing the solitary nature of the business may be, a copywriter without a pal can be like a submarine in a swimming pool. There's only so far you can go.

There's often one small addition that makes your writing better: creative chemistry.

If we do some pretend maths, I'd say that the ratio of compatibility in creative partners is about one in a thousand. Unprovable, but undoubtedly noticeable when you get into the industry. Just as Iris Murdoch (her again) wrote, albeit about a different stripe of companionship, 'to find someone – oh yes – that is the problem'.

That's not to say the majority of potential creative mates are inferior, just that your relationship with them collides with too many of the obstacles that make human beings such complicated and self-defeating creatures.

Topping the list of these obstacles is unquestionably politeness, that malignant scourge of effective and courageous ideas.

Proper creative partnerships are defined by a single characteristic - brutal, hamstring-tightening honesty.

But, if you find yourself elaborately navigating the sensitivities of your partner, or suspect they are doing the same, that hesitancy never fails to permeate the work.

And while good manners and a considerate nature make life infinitely more pleasant on crowded trains, common courtesy can be uncommonly toxic for good creative.

I'm not saying a good creative partner is the one you can abuse and bully most comprehensively. Take, for example, this snippet from Lemony Snicket's The Miserable Mill where 'Sir', the Baudelaire orphans' new guardian, declares 'I refuse to argue with you Charles! You're my partner! Your job is to iron my shirts and cook my omelettes, not boss me around.' If that kind of unequitable collaboration is your approach to the job you're majestically fucked, whoever you work with.

I'm saying that you will truly know you've found your creative match when they can tell you, quite freely, that your idea is shit – and, when they do, you feel not the mildest prickle of hurt or resentment.

Of course, a partnership founded on repeatedly rubbishing one another's thinking, however comfortable it may feel, won't be enough.

Alongside an unburdened sense of frankness, you also need to be, as it were, tickled by the same feather.

At this stage, I'll introduce my one in a thousand, a gangling, bumbling, ageing hipster who until recently dyed his hair the colour of gravy granules mixed with hot Tizer.

His name is John Clemmit, and our relationship is defined by a shared enthusiasm for unwatchable Nicolas Cage films and a series of books about a

World War Two spy who also happens to be a werewolf.

This freakish intersection of strange vices - coupled with the fact that he described one of my ideas, during our first ever job together, as like an electric toothbrush in the eye of your penis - cemented a creative relationship that needs less maintenance or nurturing than it takes to keep a tortoise alive.

Together, we disagree about a huge amount of things, make fun of each other's clothes, mercilessly denigrate one another's ability and, most importantly, produce the best creative of our careers.

There's no recipe for finding the person who compliments and completes your creativity. You can't smell their biological compatibility like monkeys. Like searching for wild honey, it's a matter of rolling up your sleeve, sticking your arm into a tree trunk and hoping you don't end up in a coma.

But, when you do find your Clemmit, you can never let him go. No matter how silly his hair looks.

COLLABORATION

Copywriting is

READING

(Or, the multiplying magic of words)

Here is where things take a slightly superfluous turn. This is where I urge you, the person reading this book to *read* books.

It's a little like giving a swimming lesson on the bottom of the ocean – anyone who needs the instruction has probably left it a little late.

But while reading this book is at least a demonstration of willingness, it's not an act of humility for me to suggest there are far more important, far more useful and far more rewarding things still to be read.

In a wonderful novel called Less by Andrew Sean Greer, the main character is a writer called Arthur Less who delivers a lecture called 'Read Like a Vampire, Write Like Frankenstein' – a perfect summary of how any copywriter can get better at what they do: suck the blood of great writing, rearrange the body parts into something new and alive.

In a rare flash of simplicity, we can safely say that reading – or at least the consumption of words – is the only way to master them.

Stephen King's book On Writing, which is as close to a holy text as a writer of any breed is likely to find, points out that reading 'offers you a constantly growing knowledge of what has been done and what hasn't, what is trite and what is fresh, what works and what just lies there dying (or dead) on the page. The more you read, the less apt you are to make a fool of yourself with your pen.'

This is every bit as true for a copywriter as it would be for a novelist. Reading (and I do mean reading way beyond our immediate world of creative copy) is where we test the originality, effectiveness and impact of our own expressions – and identify the pitfalls of cliché, self-indulgence and disingenuousness.

The only possible trap you may fall into through reading to improve your writing is if you create your own alphabetical cloister – a sealed chamber of the books, authors and words you like to read and nothing beyond.

Instead, Dorothea Brande – in Becoming a Writer – compels us to 'read with humility, determined to see the excellence in writers who are natively antipathetic to you'. Broadening our reading horizon to an author we do not know, a genre we do not appreciate or even a style of advertising we are prone to dismiss gives us a more complete understanding of what works and what doesn't, with our own preconceptions removed from the equation.

Reading also has a more immediate impact on our

copywriting – and can easily be used as the direct catalyst to unlock a tricky brief or blacken a scornfully blank page.

There's a wonderful book by the songwriter Patti Smith on the floaty and flighty nature of the creative writing process – with particular emphasis on the role reading someone else's words plays in defrosting our own.

In one passage, Smith says 'unable to write, I read', describing a fruitless spell in her own writing where she plonks herself down in a coffee shop with a copy of Patrick Modiano's Paris Nocturne and entirely abandons any attempt to force her own words out of her own mind. 'Inevitably,' writes Smith, 'somewhere midsentence, I find myself reaching for my pen'.

This is usually the stage of a chapter where I would sheepishly say something like 'of course, it's not as simple as that' and you, dear reader, would roll your eyes and wonder if I am even capable of delivering advice that wasn't draped in conditions and cautions.

Oddly, I have no such disclaimer to add in this case. Reading as a way to prompt your own writing is as close to an infallible method as you're likely to find in copywriting.

Also, what you choose to read to get yourself started is almost entirely inconsequential. If you read great and beautiful literature, the brilliance of the style and the structure offers a handy giant shoulder to perch yourself upon – for the time being.

There is, admittedly, a mild danger in reading nothing but brilliant writing. Alan Sillitoe wrote in his autobiography about becoming so lost in the 'sheer hedonism' of reading great writers that he entirely forgot to take on board anything that may make his own writing better.

Equally you must never feel like you're wasting your time by choosing anything other than 'high' literature. As George Saunders wrote in an essay called Mr Vonnegut in Sumatra 'my understanding of literature at this time was: great writing was hard reading. What made something great was you could barely understand it'. Reading may be a challenge, but it must never be a chore.

On the other end of the scale, if you read lazy and meritless advertising copy, you have given yourself the ideal point of polarity to your own efforts – i.e. do anything but this and you're doing the right thing.

A copywriter's survival kit is a sparse affair. As long as you have a notepad, a pencil, some variety of chewy fruits (wine gums preferably, midget gems if times are hard) and as many books as the fabric of your bag and body will allow, you have all you need to write something remarkable.

Copywriting is

WAITING

(Or, slow down dear, it's a commercial)

Go and read a job advert, *any* job advert, for a copywriting role. (Don't read too many at once though, that stuff is bad for you.)

Now, I am willing to wager both my elbows that the ad you read contained the phrase 'fast paced' or 'quick turnaround' or, at the very least, that old favourite 'tight deadlines'.

And fair enough. Copywriting, much like bank robbery, is the combination of imagination with momentum.

Much like Eskimos and snow, recruiters for creative agencies have a hundred different words for 'fast'.

But the word you will never find in an advert for a copywriter - or any advertising creative - is 'patience'.

Possibly this is because patience has no obvious value in an agency - i.e. you can't bill it, at least not under that name.

The more troublesome explanation is that agencies see patience as shorthand for procrastination - which, in turn, is a euphemism for slow.

But regardless of how tight the timings, how stretched the studio or how shouty the client, copywriting can rarely be done both very thoughtfully and very quickly.

Waiting is fundamental to the copywriting process.

Waiting for a good idea to come. Waiting for a good idea to reveal itself as a bad idea in a clever disguise. There is a strange alchemy in copywriting that only takes place when a line sits for a while in a closed drawer.

Putting words onto a page is easy. The worst of us can do that in a moment and still have time to half-heartedly make seven different types of fruit tea for the account team. But the craft of copywriting is more about what you do after writing.

Of course, a wonderful line may plop right out onto the page at the first attempt. But for every minute that went into writing your 'great' line, there should be another 59 making sure it really is great.

This could mean pulling its legs off. It could mean trying to write something so different to the first line they could easily get off with each other at a party and have no idea they're related. It could mean simply putting it away and letting Tomorrow You (always a more objective judge) make the call.

But in a world where creative briefs are tossed into the studio like cold chips into a crowd of seagulls, it takes a courageous writer to demand time - not just time to write words, but the time to be sure they're the right words.

So by all means tell your new copywriter how fast, how busy, how pressurised your studio will be.

But don't be surprised if they answer that it's ever so hard to build a sandcastle in a typhoon.

WAITING

Copywriting is

SOLITARY

(Or, does your imagination work in isolation?)

If, *like me*, you're not exactly a 'people person' I could cheerfully suggest a few careers you may enjoy.

A surly mountain shepherd perhaps.

Copywriting is **Solitary**. *(Or, does your imagination work in isolation?)*

A surly pearl diver. Maybe a lollipop lady on a really quiet street – providing the hi-vis doesn't detract too markedly from the appropriate degree of surliness.

Copywriting, sadly, is no place for the eremitic. From the first scratch of your pencil, through the barrelling and bruising process of agreement, to the gnawed extremities of a project, a copywriter is rarely left alone.

And, for many inspiring and important reasons, this is the way things should be. Mostly.

Creative advertising is a little like herding eels. Despite the best and most rigorous of strategic intentions, it's a process built on the unpredictability, combustibility and fundamental incompatibility between creative imagination and commercial imperative.

And, thanks to this uneasy splice, birthing an advertising concept is much like birthing a rhino calf – perilous, sticky and requiring many hands.

So a copywriter finds themselves working with a designer, an art director, an account team and ultimately a babushka nest of clients – in ascending order of authority and, unhelpfully, descending appreciation for the journey so far.

But while many young writers are grafted to creative partners from the very beginning, there remains a great deal to be said for the ability to work alone.

Yes, there are no copywriting jobs where you simply slip your words beneath the door and wait patiently for your cheque. But the ability to drive the creative beginnings of the process by yourself is impossibly valuable.

There will be times in any copywriting career, whether in the throbbing assurance of a busy agency or in the pants-and-Pringles tundra of home-working, when being able to think, write and create alone will be necessary.

And I'd urge a young writer to seize any brief opportunity to detach themselves from their significant creative other and taste this strange, and deeply satisfying, experience as early as possible.

Because, as well as the ability to generate your own ideas, you learn to manufacture your own sense of internal balance and challenge. You also get the essential, if not always pleasant, experience of fighting for your idea without another creative to absorb their share of the pummelling.

The worst state in which any copywriter can exist is in the impotence of half-ideas – shackled uncertainly to someone else's imagination while you wait for them to come and complete your thoughts.

s

Copywriting is

NOT WRITING

(Or, the importance of being idle)

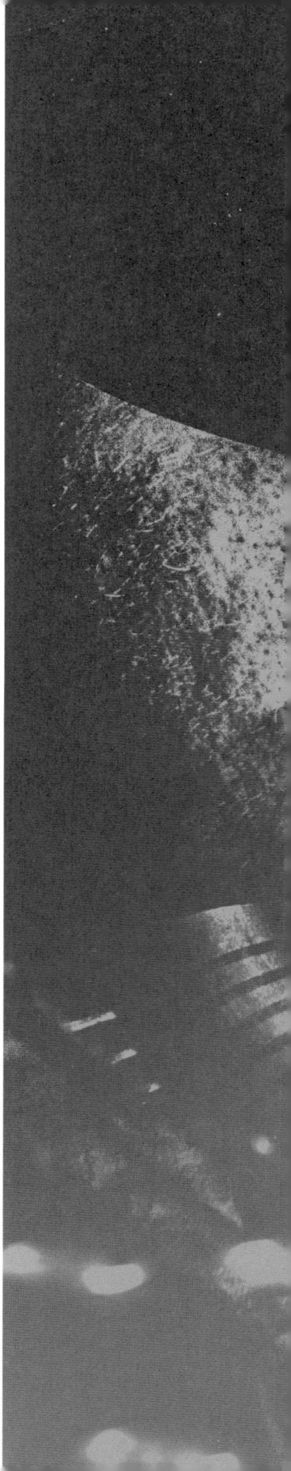

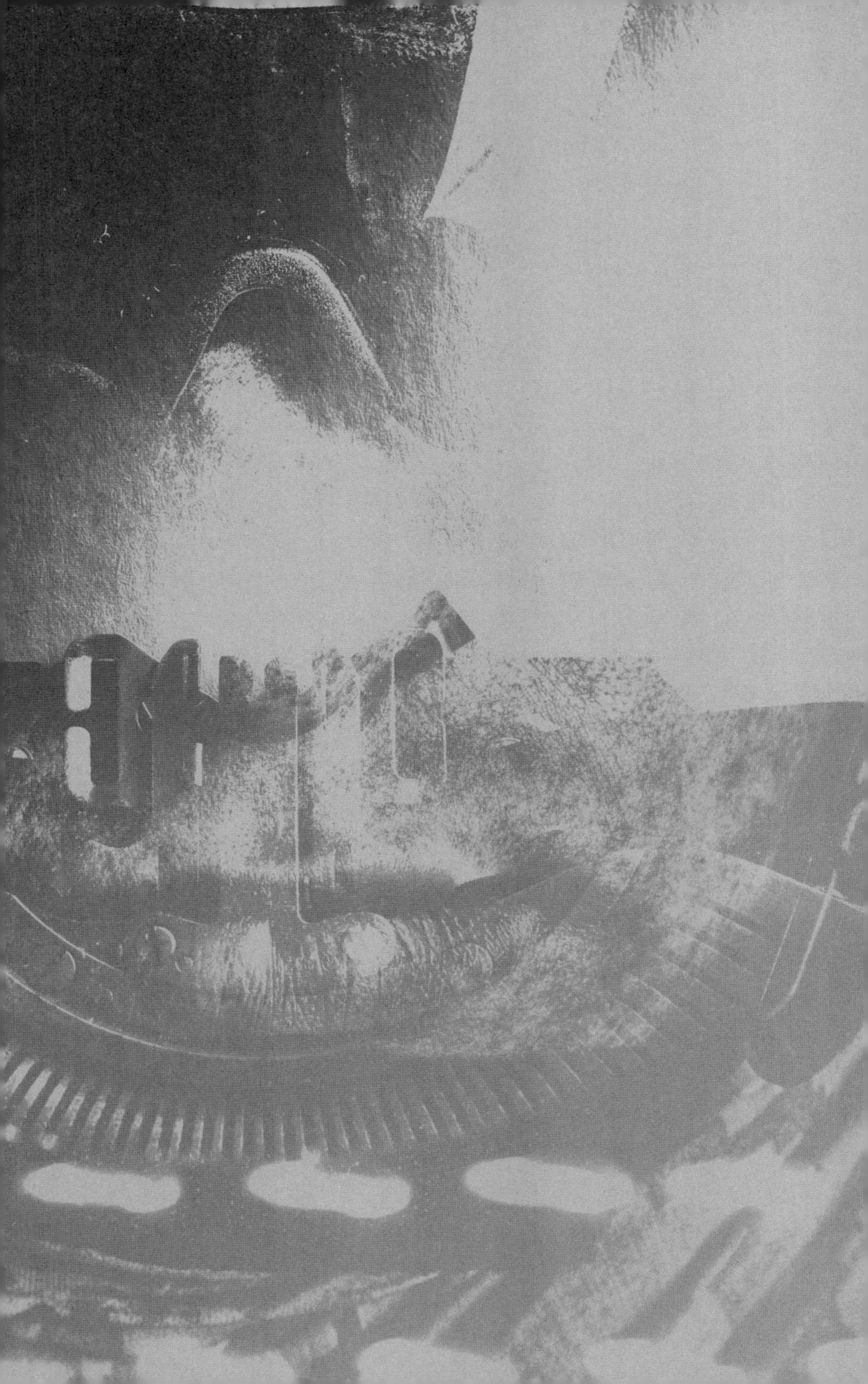

At some undefined point in time, activity and energy were promoted to the *top* of the professional food chain. Read virtually any job description for any sort of role and you will find a variation on these qualities – the subtext being that the person we want to work for us must be *seen* working for us.

And there are plenty of roles where visible industry can be linked directly to the value of your contribution. A marine who isn't climbing ropes and bayoneting sandbags is probably not marining in an acceptable way.

Our job is different, even if not everyone in the industry is prepared to see it that way.

Our value and output is not, or at least should not, be measured in how many sheets of paper we fill. Creativity is, thankfully, unweighable.

Instead, the value we bring to an agency should only be measured in terms of effectiveness and imagination - which means the way we work is impossible to evaluate in terms of how long you sit at your desk, what time you leave the office or how many typewriter ribbons you can dry out in a day.

Annoyingly, the responsibility to foster this concept in the eyes of those around, and above, you will often fall to the creative themselves. There will still be people who would happily bolt you to your desk and solder a pencil into your hand, simply because their brains are incapable of visualising any other way to work.

In a great book on the mind's strange workings called Auto Pilot, Andrew Smart perfectly describes how people, and entire business cultures, misunderstand the habits and process of creative work:

'We categorise adults who sit in contemplative moods as flaky, spacey or lazy. But for your brain to do its best work, you need to be idle. If you want to have great ideas, or if you just want to get to know yourself, you must stop managing your time.'

If, like me, you have ample skin around the middle, I'd urge you to get a tattoo of these words. If not, write them out and staple them to your skull.

What Smart describes so perfectly is a system of thinking designed to contain the infinite variations of thought. This, as Smart himself ponders, could be responsible for the loss of countless potential geniuses, whose abilities and interests were starved of air.

There is one clear and essential way copywriters can

avoid these constraints. Don't write. Or rather, don't write all the time.

Yes, people may ask you why you aren't writing, under the mistaken impression that you have been hired as a copyist rather than for your ideas.

But if you allow yourself to be harassed into writing every single moment you are in the building, you will spend most of your time straining out weak ideas and wrestling fruitlessly to disguise their flaws.

I read in Mason Curry's book, Daily Rituals, that the playwright Johann Wolfgang von Goethe – whose understanding of creativity just about trumps Tim from accounts – said that 'one should not force anything; it is better to fritter away one's unproductive days and hours, or sleep through them, than to try at such times to write something which will give one no satisfaction later on.'

And while there are few agencies prepared to indulge excessive frittering, never mind nipping off for a nap, the idea of resting your mind, or allowing it to unlock inspiration in its own way, is something we should all be asking for.

If you're asked why, then perhaps start by referring your inquisitor to the book In Praise of Slow, where Carl Honoré observes that 'a life of hurry can become superficial. When we rush, we skim the surface, and fail to make real connections with the world or other people'. This is a bad state for any human being to be in. For a copywriter it is fatal. It's not as if the only person to benefit from a bout of purposeful idleness is the writer. Roger von Oech points out that, by placing your ideas on a 'mental back burner', you are taking advantage of three distinct factors which will improve that idea:

1. You put the problem in perspective (you are so close to it, it's impossible to see the solution)

2. When you work on a problem you plant a seed in your mind. When you back away, this seed continues to grow.

3. When you return to an idea after allowing it to incubate, you'll approach it with different assumptions.

Creative solutions rarely fall from the sky, but they can never be dragged into existence purely because your working hours demand it.

The hardest working copywriters do everything they can to find that startling idea. And the smartest of those realise that includes doing absolutely nothing all.

Copywriting is

PROPER WRITING

(Or, learn from literature...
even if you're selling lawnmowers)

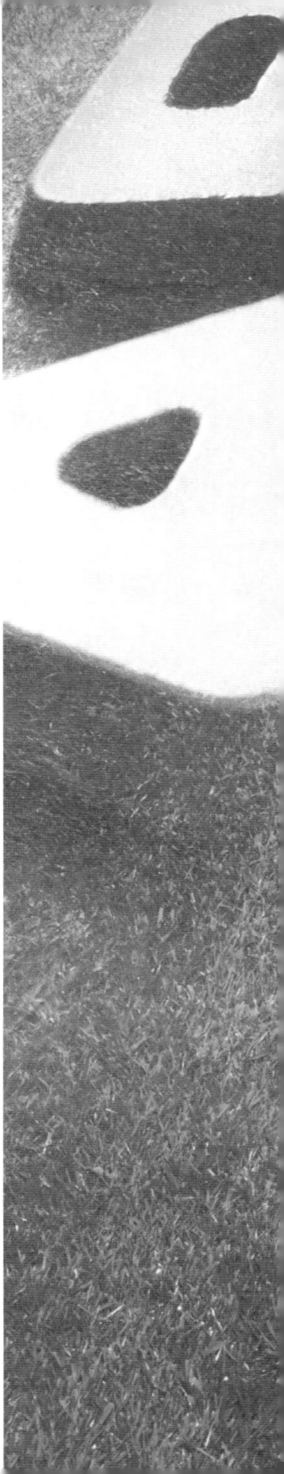

When people ask me what I do I tend to say 'copywriter' and brace myself for the prolonged, *awkward* explanation. Occasionally, I'll simply say 'writer' and brace myself for the crippling self-disgust.

And yet, the more closely you examine the intersection between writing for art and writing for sales, the more shared experience, anxiety and methods you will find.

Survey the desk space of copywriters throughout the land and, aside from a jumbo packet of own-brand Jaffa Cakes, I'd imagine the most common adornment you'll find is a copy of Orwell's rules for writing stuck to the wall.

It makes perfect sense. Orwell's rules, though perhaps designed for something more towering than the back of a cereal box, are a superb checklist for copywriters – a guide by which to measure the clarity and quality of our work, with a telling reminder about flexibility and the use of judgement.

There are several so-called rules for the literary world that can help a copywriter develop their craft. The theatrical principle known as Chekov's Gun states that everything we write must have significance – namely, if you see a gun in the first act it must go off in the third. For a medium like ours, where purpose and persuasion are the main concerns, a rule that demands the efficiency of our words is deeply relevant.

Likewise, Roddy Doyle's quip about keeping your thesaurus in a shed or behind the fridge – 'somewhere that demands travel or effort' – is a handsome piece of copywriting advice. Doyle's belief that the word you think of first is most often the best is reinforced by the kind of anxious copy that reads as if every word has been ground through the synonym sausage machine.

I would, however, agree that a copywriter should be wary of too rigorously applying literary principles to our process. For example, a common novelist's tip is to trust a reader to arrive at the desired conclusion with the slenderest possible direction. In reality, the majority of copywriting briefs require precisely the opposite approach.

And yet, with a discerning eye, there is much to be plucked from the authors, the screenwriters and the dramatists.

Simple principles like cut until you can cut no more, or read voraciously, or never leave home without a notebook are the foundations for anyone hoping to exchange words for shiny objects. Elmore Leonard's decree that you are allowed two or three exclamation points per 100,000 words would certainly make the copywriting realm a less giddy and disingenuous space. Cormac McCarthy's belief 'in periods, in capitals, in the occasional comma, and that's it' at least removes the worry over how and where and why a semi-colon should appear.

I suppose if I had to pick a favourite rule I would paraphrase a man with a particular genius for scattering the alphabet on the page, W Somerset Maugham: there are three rules for copywriting. Unfortunately, no one knows what they are.

PROPER WRITING

Copywriting is

ENVY

(Or, why a bit of creative cannibalism is a good thing)

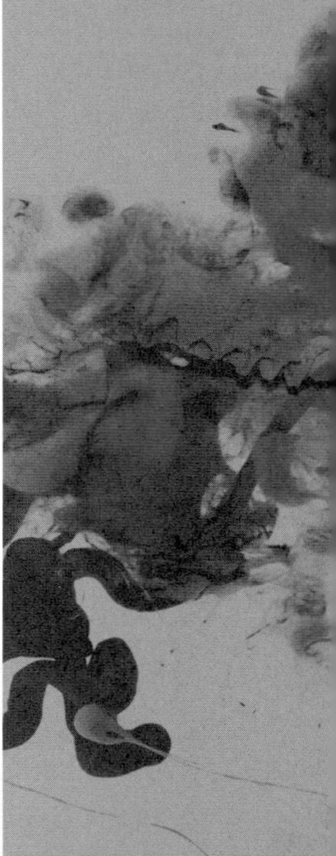

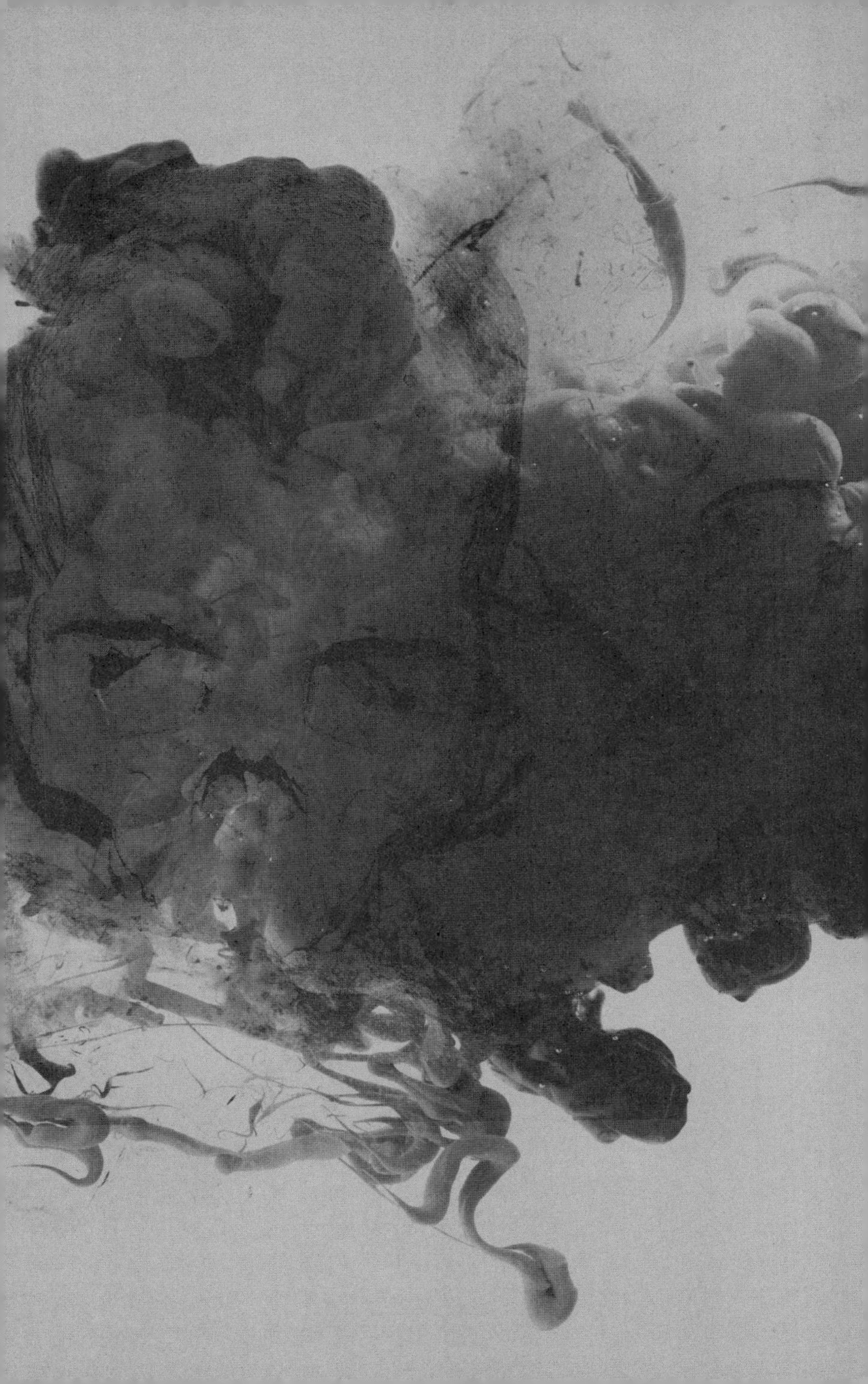

Copywriting, in its dark, *inky* heart, is a jealous business. Few of us have never experienced the piercing jab of professional envy at a fellow writer's brilliance.

Most of us, I suspect, are pierced so frequently that if you dropped us into water we'd percolate like a teabag.

Such a covetous approach to work could easily be debilitating. Allow yourself to be pummelled too frequently by the excellent things you aren't doing and you could find yourself desperately adrift from any excellent things you could be doing.

And yet the idea of envy as a wholly destructive emotion comes from the same primary school morality that teaches you to share your toys, write within the lines and carry your remainders.

In reality, envy can be a powerful and positive emotion for any copywriter. We exist, after all, in a tunnel of inspiration – and by necessity must first draw in the things that inspire us before we can expel the things that will inspire our reader.

Naturally that inspiration will come from words. And though inspiring writing is hardly in short supply, a copywriter who fails to properly filter their inspiration quickly blurs the distinction between poetic and persuasive.

It makes perfect sense then that our creative inspiration should primarily be guzzled directly from copywriting's own swollen udders.

And it's a churlish and self-defeating copywriter who sees taking inspiration from great copy as an affront to their originality.

On the contrary, seeing the very best example of the kind of line you're hoping to write, is a wholly constructive way to begin your process. Firstly, it gives you the highest possible bar against which to measure your own efforts (which is a remarkably effective way to filter out weary lines that a less critical eye might have been willing to submit).

More importantly, disassembling the elements that make a great line of copy so effective is like a map to a more compelling solution. Following someone else's impeccable reasoning is not cheating (and it won't end with you ripping off the line that inspired you in the first place). Like a computer game cheat code from the 1980s, it will merely carry you over the hazards and plonk you down on a more rewarding path.

Envy is a daily part of my own copywriting process. I'll seek out the lines and ideas that make me want to break my pencil-holding hand and start a new life emptying dog-poo bins in the park. But, I'll invariably find something in that annoyingly flawless copy to help me create something better – or at least, better than a page of work that can be measured against nothing more rigorous than itself.

Now, this is not to say that copywriting must fall into a withering loop of cannibalistic voyeurism – peering over our neighbour's shoulder while we pucker ourselves into a human centipede.

Copywriting, like most creative occupations, has a nasty habit of making a fetish of the past – devotedly gobbling the flakes from the shoulders of giants. But, as long as the inspiration we take is fuel for imagination, not imitation, there's nothing wrong with seeing an ad, wishing you'd thought of it and (perhaps, just a tiny bit) hating the clever fucker who did.

NV

Copywriting is

LIMITATIONS

(Or, learn to love the box)

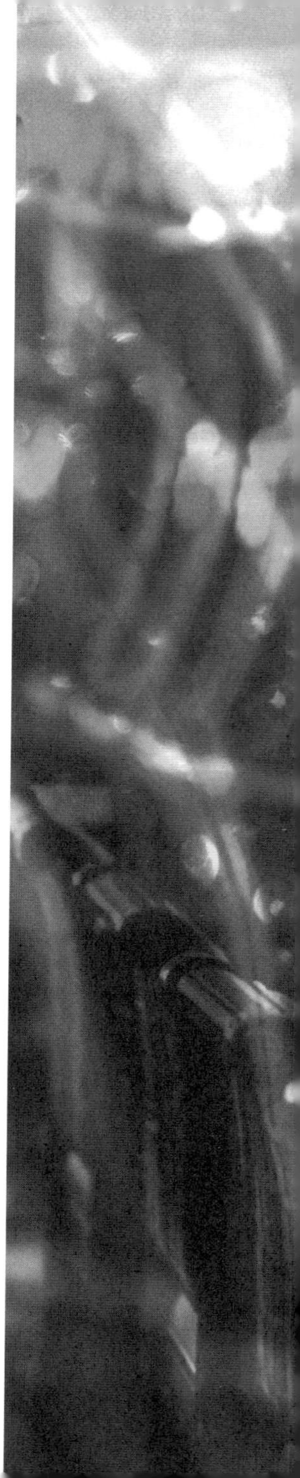

My first ever paid writing assignment was writing *football* match reports for a newspaper in Sydney. (On an unrelated note, I had no TV and had to go and sit in an all-night casino to watch the matches which, while entirely pleasant, would also leave me with around minus forty dollars as my net pay.)

The first report I filed came in rather cleanly at around 600 words. Which, given the fluidity of my prose, the originality of my observations and an indulgent aside about my own schoolboy football days, was pretty much the finest piece of sports writing ever produced. Apart from the minor niggle that I had overshot my word count by 480 words.

It was my first taste of limitation in writing, as well as my first experience of how furious Australian sports editors can get.

In copywriting there will be no occasions where you are able to work free of such restrictions. Sometimes they may feel generous, sometimes adequate, sometimes arbitrary and entirely impossible. But never will there be a brief without them.

At first you will find these limitations rather, well, limiting. How preposterous, you will splutter to your fellows, that you are being hired for the dazzling expanse of your imagination while being judged on the compactness of your solution.

What you will hopefully learn is that these two states are not incompatible. Better still, you will discover a direct relationship between the quality of the work and the tininess of the space in which it will exist.

John Yorke, in a magnificent book on the writing process called Into The Woods, quotes a famous old line from the author GK Chesterton – 'Art consists of limitation. The most beautiful part of every picture is the frame'.

The same can be said, perhaps more loudly, about copywriting. Our craft is about immediacy, about the ability to tell entire stories to people who have neither the time nor interest to hear them. And five startling words will do a far better job of arresting your audience than two hundred words of any standard.

That isn't to say copywriters are only there to make things shorter. We are there to take the space we have been given and add purpose and value to every square inch. This doesn't mean we cheat the word count by flooding our ad from top to bottom with everything we need to say, it means perfectly forming every component of your message so you can make the greatest impact with the fewest words. As the author James Baldwin declared, 'you want to write a sentence as clean as a bone'.

Embracing the limitations of the form marks the difference between a copywriter who is in control of their story and space and one who can only fulfil one of these requirements at a time.

'Limitations can be liberating' says Frances Ambler in her excellent book for the Tate, On Creativity. 'Setting limits not only gives you a place to start, it also encourages you to push your work as far as possible... with new limits and new challenges come new horizons.'

It may surprise you to discover that openness and freedom are more stifling than a brief that fences you in. It's a form of creative agoraphobia where the challenge becomes more daunting and misdirecting the further you get from the edge – like a swimmer who could swim mile after mile in a pool, thrashing about in the middle of the sea.

Learn to love your boxes and you'll learn to take far more satisfaction from working within them. A sprawling space encourages your writing to sprawl as well, and no copywriter in the history of advertising has ever been able to measure the value of the work by weighing it.

LMTNS.

Copywriting is

IMMEDIACY

(Or, think drama, not dawdle)

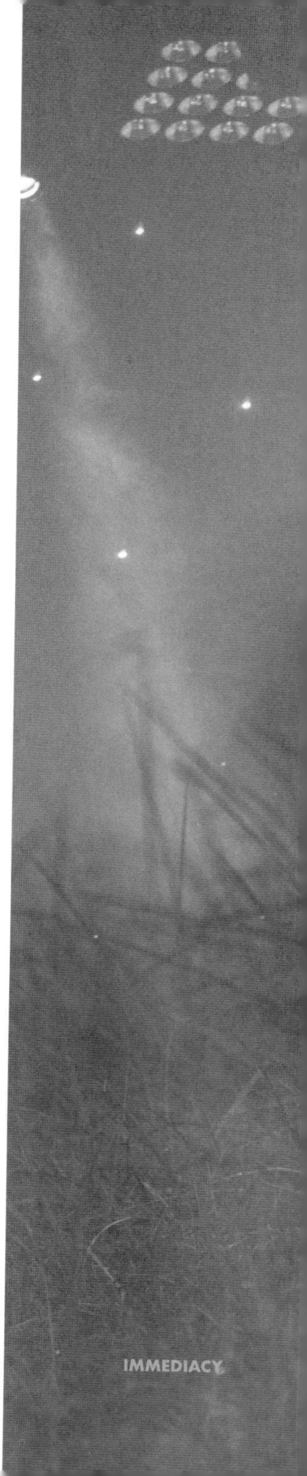

If you are any stripe of writer and there is *nothing* you can learn from Nora Ephron you are either:

A. Not really a writer.

Or

B. A writer so impossibly brilliant it feels unfair, if not downright malicious, for you to write another remarkable word before the rest of us have had a chance to catch up.

Now that we've filtered out those who have no need for Nora, we're free to take in a little of her wisdom on the craft of writing.

Ephron once put together a list of 6 rules for writing a news magazine cover story, a task she was confident could be completed without having to rely on impracticalities such as facts, talent or imagination.

All six points are worth your attention, but in this case I think number five best illustrates the theme of this chapter:

'5. Use statistics where possible. Better yet, use statistics so mind boggling that no reader will bother with simple arithmetic to determine their impossibility.'

As a way to obscure your meaning, curtail your story and squander your readers' precious attention, you cannot do much better than rule number five.

And while such obvious padding and evasion is irritating in journalism, it is catastrophic in copywriting.

There is only one thing you need to say in your copy, and that is the thing you need to say. The trick, however, is knowing what needs to be said and what should be left unsaid - and, of course, what may still be said without actually having to say it. As such. Simple, no?

There is a temptation secreted deep in a copywriter's bones toward exposition - to set the scene, to plug every gap and anticipate every question. It is as understandable as it is fatal, and is easily the most well-intentioned way to bore your audience to death.

Copywriting, in terms of style, structure and concept, may be many, many things. In terms of its delivery it is only allowed to be one thing - immediate.

In William Noble's wonderful guide to better writing, Show Don't Tell, his advice is for writers not to 'creep up' on their story. His instruction to 'start your copy halfway down the page' is as true for our kind of writing as it is for any other. Noble says 'When we begin a story, we should be ready to throw out the first few sentences or paragraphs in order to get things going' - which, in a copywriter's world could mean throwing out everything apart from the one phrase, or even one word, that becomes more luminous, more powerful and more persuasive the fewer companions it has on the page.

Noble draws on a superb example from the literary world, the words of novelist Phyllis Whitney who said 'perhaps the best, and safest beginning is for the writer to present immediately someone interesting doing something interesting.' How many copywriters, I wonder, regardless of their success or experience, start their copy with such a direct path between our brief and our audience.

A common anxiety around this is to ask what happens to the idea of tension or suspense or subverted expectations if we have to land everything in a single blow.

I say there doesn't necessarily need to be a choice between tension and immediacy. Tension has a role to play in copywriting under the right circumstances, which may often be in a longer form of copy.

Consider this from Ray Bradbury in Zen in the Art of Writing:

'We build tensions toward laughter; then give permission and laughter comes.
We build tensions toward sorrow, and at last say cry and hope to see our audience in tears.

We build tensions toward violence, light the fuse and run.
We build the strange tensions of love, where so many of the other tensions mix to be modified and transcended, and allow that fruition in the minds of the audience.

We build tensions, especially today, toward sickness and then, if we are good enough, talented enough, observant enough, allow our audiences to be sick. Each tension seeks its own proper end, release and relaxation.'

Reading this, you'd be appalled if such a dramatic and memorable technique was banned from a copywriting brief. And of course it isn't – providing your tension is a.) not needlessly or indulgently drawn-out and b.) that it is designed solely to soften up your reader for the delivery of the knock-out thought. Not perhaps, then, immediacy in its truest form – but immediacy we invite our reader to discover for themselves.

After all, it is neither lofty nor delusional to say that copywriting is drama. Your words must transport an audience to a different state - without the luxury of them having bought a ticket to watch your story unfold.

Copy demands dramatic effect, and dramatic effect in copy requires a complete and compelling thought to infiltrate your readers' minds - before they've had a chance to blink away your ad. It is our equivalent of what John Mullan, author of How Novels Work, says about a novel's duty to 'establish its contract with its reader' - and in our case that contract must be built around the understanding of a need and the relevance of a solution.

It is ok if a reader needs to think about your copy. It is never ok if it needs explaining to them.

Copywriting is

SELECTION

(Or, choosing your words ruthlessly)

For a very public and *brutal* assessment of your ability, nothing beats playground football. For those of you unfamiliar with the process – you lucky, unbroken bastards – it works a little like this:

Two members of the class are assigned as captains. Occasionally this role is awarded for utilitarian reasons, for example, the bringer of the ball. Mostly, however, it is allocated under the harshest evolutionary terms to the popular kids, the big kids, and the kids too tough and unpredictable to welcome a discussion over democratic principles. What these leaders offer in terms of status, talent, physicality or knuckle size, is generally offset by a distinct absence of compassion and discretion.

Therefore, when it comes to picking teams, there is no concession given to feelings. If you are judged to be fast, big, strong, skilful enough by these scab-kneed Stalins, you are picked. If all you have to offer is a pure heart and asthmatic lungs, you are not.

It is an unpleasant way to learn about your standing amongst peers. It is an equally unpleasant way to join a team, knowing full well that if the other child at the bottom of the draft didn't have both narcolepsy and rickets you mightn't have been picked at all. But while the playground parade of your weaknesses does little for self-esteem, it's a method that every copywriter should be looking to incorporate.

Correct me if I'm wrong, but I can't think of a single copywriter who began their career with a fully formed sense of ruthlessness. I don't mean ruthless in the way some writers will spike your hazelnut latte with whizz 30 minutes before you meet the ECD. I mean ruthless in the way they deal with words.

One of the many odd paradoxes of being a copywriter is that you probably got into it through a love of words – but will only ever succeed by thrashing them until they whimper.

Copywriting, I believe, is that rare writing profession where there is no room for alphabetical indulgence. A delicious phrase that doesn't in any way advance the plot can probably still make it into your novel, if you're willing to out-tantrum your publisher. A spot of lofty self-puffery can creep into a newspaper article, if you make a tactical, too-late-to-change submission. But in copywriting, every word must be chosen to do a job that no other word can do.

John McPhee, in his excellent book, Draft No. 4, observes, 'writing is selection. Just to start a piece of writing you have to choose one word and only one from more than a million in the language'. This being the case, we find ourselves in the uncomfortable (ok, secretly triumphant) position of playground team captain. Words are lined up before us, sweating and shuffling and hoping to be picked or, at the very least, not publicly mortified. There goes poor 'discover', unpicked again, weeping into the dinner lady's spongy hips.

What's more, unlike the break-time captains, we actually have to turn our selected players into a cohesive team. Picking thirty goal-thirsty glory-boys may work in football matches that regularly end in eighty-all draws, but a copywriter's choice demands a more balanced and complementary selection.

Developing this ruthlessness first demands you formulate a more severe set of criteria for what your words must do. Brad Blanton writes, in Radical Honesty, 'language has the power to evoke the being of human beings and rescue them from their own minds'. If something like this becomes the expectation you set for your chosen words, you clearly have no option than to choose more discerningly.

That's the power a copywriter has and must be prepared to wield. Even when it leaves your most darling words standing on the sidelines, bitterly willing someone to hoof your ball into a tree.

S|E|L|E|C|T|I|O|N

Copywriting is

EFFORTLESS

(Or, The Gosling Effect)

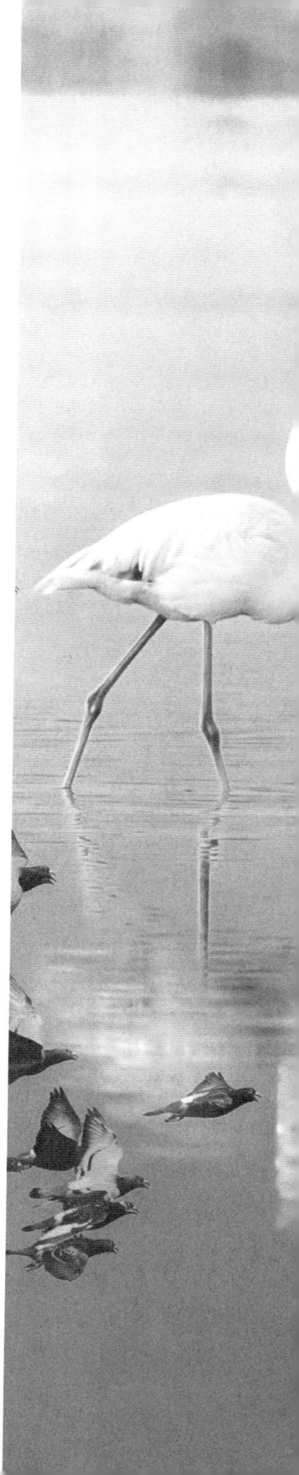

Why do people fancy Ryan Gosling? Apart from his impeccable suits, flawlessly rumpled hair and eyes that make your leg bones feel like chewed ham, *what is it?*

*Copywriting is **Effortless**. (Or, The Gosling Effect)*

It's the fact that his intense handsomeness is all so effortless. What he can convey in a lazy blink would demand so much effort from a man like me I'd probably vomit up my own pelvis.

This impression of ease is terribly handy if you're a slightly off-key movie heartthrob – but it's positively priceless if you're a copywriter.

Good copywriting, if I were to truss it up in an unsteady metaphor, is a wink amongst screams.

The very finest work to emerge from our profession demonstrates the tremendously persuasive force of alphabetical poise – the sheer throbbing urgency that can be conveyed by a string of languorous letters.

You see, people can sniff out an ad. They taste it on the air like damp grass in a hot car and, frankly, it pisses them off. Flannery O'Connor wrote in an essay that 'every now and then the novelist looks up from his work long enough to become aware of the general public dissatisfaction with novelists.' With copywriters and advertising, often, we don't look up at all.

What gives most ads and marketing messages away is the sour, trembling panic of their words. The ferocious need to be noticed gushes from these headlines like hot sick from a bin pigeon. They are obvious, insincere, intrusive and, invariably, ignored.

But effortless copy has a very different effect. It strides into a stranger's day with confidence, attaching no conspicuous purpose to its presence other than to entice. It is the murmured ending to a wildly successful joke that convinces us we must stand closer to the teller.

Above all, the effortless copy line is the one that reverses the natural trajectory of competitive advertising. While most advertising language is designed to shove its way into your line of sight, effortless copy invites your eyes to come closer. The first is a business of clamour and obstacles, but the second is a tantalising orbit of naked human curiosity.

But of course few things in our profession require such concentrated effort as producing something that sounds unforced. The infuriating reality is that, for most of us, such beguiling breeziness is not achieved with our feet on the desk, a champagne flute in one hand and a pencil dangling blithely from the other.

Rather, the effortless line is one that has been hammered into a state of repose like cheap, tough brisket. However casually it may seem to lounge across the page, you and I know it is propped up by the boiled skulls of its flappier forebears.

A dead giveaway for a failed bid at effortless writing is the piss-stink of the thesaurus on your page. It is not possible to come across as unruffled when carelessly implanted words ruffle everything they touch. This is what Ursula K Le Guin calls the 'dictionary word, the word that really isn't your word, may stick out of your prose like a flamingo in a flock of pigeons.' Reeking of effort.

Instead, a good indicator of whether you have written an effortlessly effective piece of copy is when people glance at it, nod, smile and say nothing else. It takes distance to appreciate the effortlessness in our own messages, but we are at least in control of the parts that feel too noisy, too needy, too obviously taking more than it gives back.

So next time you're pasting new pictures and poems into your Ryan Gosling pop-up 'crush book' just remember how hard you have to try to appear as if you haven't.

Copywriting is

SMALL

(Or, be more piranha)

Our business has
a fixation with *big*.
Big ideas, big impact,
big returns.

And while this is, mostly, a useful measure of our output it can be misleading in terms of how we arrive there.

Tackling a brief with enormous bites can give you terrible creative indigestion. Some problems simply refuse to be swallowed whole.

And yet, pretty much every copywriter who has ever chewed a pencil will have learned this the hard way.

The trouble with starting big is that it leaves you nowhere else to go. I've started to answer many briefs with grand and unwieldy ideas and then, when it's too late, discovered they are either needlessly complex or riddled with holes.

There is an obvious solution to this - think small.

I don't mean you should rein in your ambition or aim for anything less than a startlingly good solution. I just mean you should tiptoe your way to it, rather than going for the audacious leap from beginning straight to glorious end.

The smallness of your approach should also start way before you scribble your first line. It should begin when you're trying to find the surprising and compelling truth about your audience that will make your idea work.

'Observation doesn't have to be about volume. The slightest things work' says Michael Atavar in Everyone is Creative, and he's absolutely right.

Much of the time you will be asked to improve the lives of your audience in the tiniest ways. Outcomes like pointing someone in the direction of a tastier fizzy drink or a slightly more comfortable headphone.

Your response to such challenges needs to reflect the nature and size of the problem. Treating such a task like you've been asked to make pigeons sexier will lead you to dramatically overshoot the remit of your brief. A smaller, but truer, understanding of the realities of that problem will bring you far closer to something your audience will want to hear.

If your problem does happen to be particularly sprawling and complex, there's a process Peter Sims describes, in his book Little Bets, as 'smallifying', where you break down the challenge into smaller, and relatively simpler, problems.

Either way, the method is about making the task in front of you seem more creatively manageable, and therefore more likely to yield to your imagination.

If your brief is a two-thousand pound elk, think of yourself as a piranha. Munching it down in one gulp is going to cause you a great deal of jaw strain, while the elk will barely notice it's on the menu.

But take smaller and more significant bites and, with a bit of logic and patience, you'll soon be swimming around with a pile of bones and a belly full of ideas.

John Maeda's first law of simplicity is to do with 'thoughtful reduction' - in other words, asking yourself how simple can you make it and how complex does it need to be.

One way to make a racing bicycle as light as possible is to remove the water bottle, seat padding and brakes. But, while it's undoubtedly lighter, its rider is unlikely to win many races when chronically dehydrated, suffering from crippling haemorrhoids and liable to smash into a tree at any point.

There are things you can remove in any brief to make the problem narrower and more focussed. But equally, there are things that, if removed, fundamentally change the nature of the brief and the direction you will follow to solve it.

Understanding what matters most and what is superfluous is the most effective way to make your problem smaller while still making sure you're providing the solution you've been asked to find.

In other words, it takes small steps to arrive at a big idea. At least, it does if you want your idea to work.

SMALL

Copywriting is

EXPLODING

(Or, for god's sake get it out)

At some point in your copywriting career, no matter how much you resist, you will find yourself doing a little move I like to call the *One Word Rub*.

Not quite as grubby it sounds, it simply means you'll write the first word of your copy, immediately rub it out, start again, rub out again and so forth until you've wasted an entire morning birthing and then slaughtering a single word that, for some reason, doesn't meet your requirements.

It's an agonising way to write, though entirely understandable. No one who alphabets for a living likes the idea of starting badly. Something in our brains tells us that writing is a flat-terrain pastime, possibly even a downhill sport. If our beginning is weak, then that is the altitude we have assigned to the entirety of the piece.

But of course, this is not true. Some writers would even happily argue that the shittiness of their first draft is a necessity if they are to later produce anything of value.

Anne Lamott, in Some Instructions on Writing and Life, refers to the first draft as 'the child's draft'. It is 'where you let it all pour out and then let it romp all over the place, knowing that no one is going to see it and that you can shape it later.'

That absence of doubt, plus resisting the urge to live-critique your efforts allows you to get words on the page – words that don't have to, and never will be, the right ones in the right order, but that can be addressed later.

The key to effective copywriting is to remember that writing and editing are separate processes. They cannot overlap.

Instead, by treating your first sitting of writing as a consequence-free opportunity to splurge, you are at least ensuring the editor half of your brain will have something to get stuck into.

By far the most useful piece of writing advice I have ever read comes not from a fellow copywriter but from the novelist Ray Bradbury. He says this:

'Hot today, cool tomorrow. This afternoon, burn down the house. Tomorrow, pour cold critical water upon the simmering coals. Time enough to think and cut and re-write tomorrow. But today – explode – fly apart – disintegrate.'

That act of explosion contains enough force, fire and

deafening noise to distract you from any doubts, or the urge to find fault with everything you put onto the page.

Today's you is in charge only of splattering the walls with imagination. Tomorrow you is the one who has to tidy it up.

G

I N

D

O

L

P

X

E

Copywriting is

FUCKING UP

(Or, having the confidence to get it wrong)

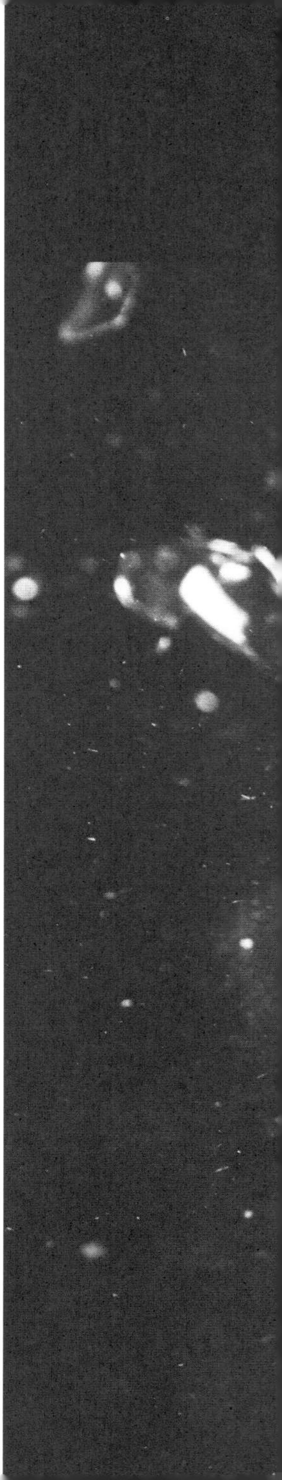

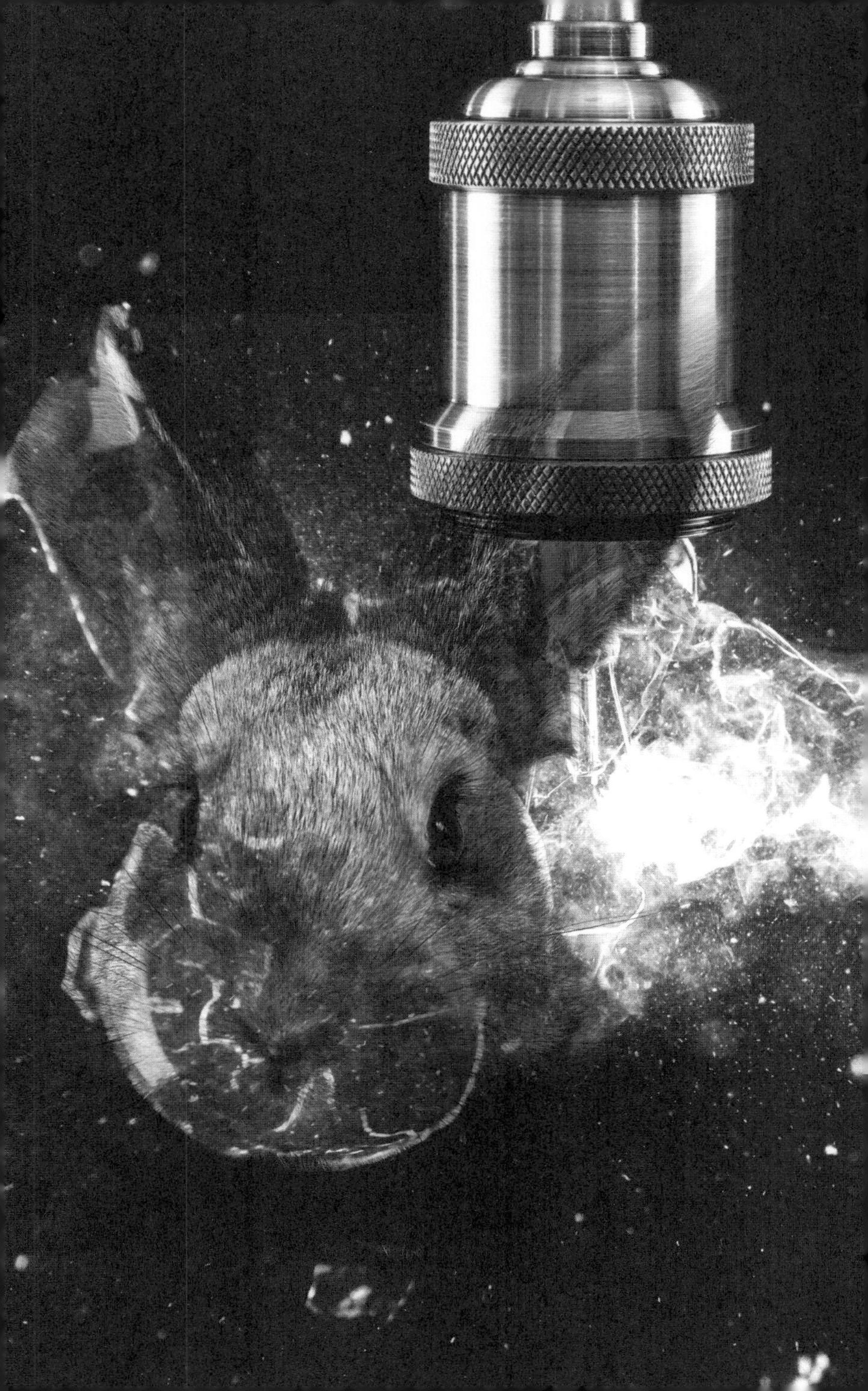

It is not ok to make mistakes as a copywriter – it is *essential.*

While some jobs may ask for immediate success, ours is one that feeds on failure. The bumps in the road don't get in the way of where we're going, they merely adjust the direction of where it is we need to go.

In other words, I urge you to fuck up. Fuck up big and fuck up small. Fuck up with great regularity, and if you suspect you may not yet have fucked up, you must look harder for a way to do so.

'Some ideas are born ugly' says David Hieatt in Why: Brands With Purpose, and if you approach any copywriting brief aiming only for instant and unquestionable perfection your best ideas are likely to lie in the bottom of your bin, their potential brilliance entirely untested.

The most frequently cited evidence for the fucking up method is Thomas Edison, inventive genius and the reason you're not reading this by candlelight right now.

John Ingledew, in another excellent book that touches on the scruffiness of the creative process, How To Have Great Ideas, writes about Edison's 10,000 unsuccessful prototypes for the lightbulb – and his marvellous assertion that he has not failed a single time but rather succeeded in proving those 10,000 ways will not work.

Your copy is your lightbulb. The likelihood of you arriving at the perfect solution at the first time of asking is beyond slim. The tricky part is not letting these missteps feel like failures but rather necessary steps to a better solution.

In fact, an excellent way to arrive at a surprising and effective line is by writing as many unsurprising and ineffective lines as you can think of. See what the weak solutions look like and you learn a great deal about which way your copy should be facing.

And while spotting the mistakes in our own creative is pretty much the only fool-proof path to improvement, spotting the mistakes in other people's creative also allows us to sidestep manholes before we plunge down them ourselves. Sol Stein, the legendary author, publisher and editor talks about 'the necessity of sitting through bad plays'. There is extraordinary creative value, he says, in being there...

'...to witness the coughing and squirming in the audience, to have ears up like a rabbit to catch what didn't work, to observe how little tolerance an audience has for a mishap'.

Yet, whether we are dealing with our own fuck ups or somebody else's, there is often an unwillingness to acknowledge the value in error. Melanie Rothschild wrote a wonderful book on the power of creative missteps, The Art of Mistakes, in which she imagines not only what creativity would look like without mistakes, but how life itself would appear. For her, 'the entire evolutionary process rests on a dance of mistakes and new directions.'

That dance is one we're unable to sit out. Creative mistakes will come no matter what we do to guard against them. Creativity, after all, is a leap across a river. The only guarantee of staying dry is to never leap. Rothschild says:

'Mistakes give us ideas that we could never deliberately think up otherwise. Yet we are misguidedly programmed to steer clear of them... at all costs. And most of the time, the price we pay for avoiding mistakes is the cost of stretching our thinking in substantive, new ways. There are serious consequences for not understanding the nature of how mistakes serve us.'

And for me, that's the most important point of all. It's not the mistakes that harm us as creative thinkers, but an unwillingness to look them in the eye.

My only other advice on how to fuck up like an expert is this. Don't be in a rush to undo every mistake. Simply changing one thing with each new version you produce helps you see how your message might unfold. You may even discover that, with an adjustment to the North of your page, the previously ugly inhabitants in the South suddenly make a lot more sense.

Your fuck ups don't have to be in the public domain if that makes you uneasy. Fucking up can be a private enterprise if you prefer, leaving you free to present an extraordinary solution that nobody else knows is version forty-seven of the idea.

But, for me, I always choose to share the horrors I encountered on the way to a good line, because taking people along the same rutted and rudderless journey I stumbled through gives them a greater appreciation of the ultimate destination. Like stowing away in the Megabus toilet on your way to a spa retreat.

We are copywriters and we are fuck-ups. And it's impossible to do the first with skill without being able to do the second with confidence.

Copywriting is

DISAGREEABLE

(Or, nice copywriting finishes last)

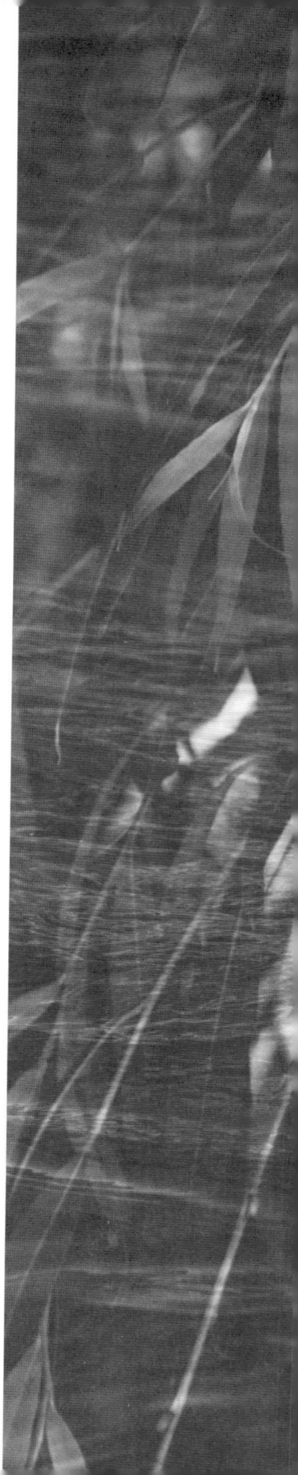

The copywriters I know are *nice*. They have soft hands and smell like willow trees and Maltesers.

In the event of a hurricane, they would paddle canoes from bungalow to bungalow rescuing old ladies and their damp cats.

But the very best copywriters I know are also entirely disagreeable.

It's a form of disagreeability that doesn't manifest in the usual ways. It isn't the sort of prickling hostility you see quarrelling with car park attendants or being noisy in the cinema.

Instead, it's a wilful, thoughtful sort, one that refuses to regard the map and the journey as the same thing.

To a copywriter, a disagreeable approach feeds invention. It's the vast, unruly fabric from which the most original thoughts are cut.

Malcolm Gladwell says all innovators depend on a fundamentally disagreeable nature. Not obnoxious as such, but 'willing to take social risks – to do things that others might disapprove of.'

Copywriting, like any other branch of invention, is the pursuit of a new truth. At its most potent it is a radical act, a transformation of human understanding. Tearing apart a cardigan and re-stitching it as a parachute.

This demands that certain conventions should be challenged. And copywriting, or perhaps creative advertising as a whole, can be notoriously shackled to convention.

Ours is a business that makes a fetish out of its own beginnings. Turning the methods and beliefs of its founding fathers into a dogma they were never supposed to be.

Similarly, copywriting is curiously fond of digging its own trenches before the creative process has begun – mapping a terrain of language that already exists and finding a way to squeeze one more voice into the din.

But the best copywriting – the work we envy as keenly as we remember – is usually the stuff that seems oblivious to the canon. Like a new writer on a TV soap who has no knowledge of the plot or characters and so transfers all the action to a moon colony.

Disagreeable copywriting is the work that sees the difference between the way things should be done, the way they have been done and they way they could be done. It's the writer who, attacked by a shark, punches themselves on the nose just to change the rules of the fight.

It's not easy to be creatively contrary, to replant a conversation whose roots have been buried in the same spot for decades.

But then if it was easy, it wouldn't be that disagreeable would it?

DISAGREEABLE

Copywriting is

SOPHISTICATION

(Or, the dangers of dumbing down)

You know you're *finished* as a writer when you begin a chapter with a dictionary definition.

So, the dictionary tells us that 'sophistication' means *'finely experienced and aware, intellectually appealing'*. (A second meaning is to do with complexity of design, but that doesn't fit my point so will be ignored.)

Now, were we all to write down on Post-It notes the single word that best defines copywriting, we would have enough small, sticky pieces of paper to camouflage an oil rig.

And, broadly speaking, none of these words would be wrong. It's just, for me, nothing encapsulates good copywriting more than sophistication.

Talk to some clients about a sophisticated solution and they may mishear what you're saying as lofty or inaccessible. But sophistication has nothing to do with impenetrable, over-intellectualised writing - it's to do with a fine and focussed sense of purpose.

Sophisticated copy doesn't require you to use big words. It doesn't require you to use many words at all. It simply asks you to use words that engage your reader's brain. As Nassim Nicholas Taleb says 'charm lies in the unsaid, the unwritten and the undisplayed. It takes mastery to control silence'. This mastery, and in many ways this silence, is what I talk about when I talk about sophisticated copywriting.

As a group we are deviantly unrepresentative of the wider audience - word perverts, lurking at tube platforms, though never boarding any train. Mind-wanking to alphabetical smut across the tracks.

Yet, invariably the copy that works hardest, speaks clearest and lingers longest is that which bears the hallmark of sophistication.

That sophistication can be asking someone to see revelation in the familiar. It can be a demonstration of understanding. It can simply be the precise pinballing of recognition into reflection into action.

Copy, unless it's destined for the bulging quarries of creative landfill, should appeal to the intellect - not in the way watching QI or pretending to read Finnegans Wake does, but in a way that wins the brain's attention and rewards it with something to nibble on.

Sophistication is easy to detect in your copywriting. Done right and you can practically smell a reader's brain gleefully sautéing what you put in front of them. Done wrong, and you'll discover human faces are not designed to effectively disguise apathy.

Kindly do not read this as permission to write your copy in a ball gown, or search the internet for velvet pencils (not a euphemism). It is simply my observation that, if we're going to do this strange, scruffy, gnawed-pencil of a job, let's at least do it with some class.

Sophistication

Copywriting is

RHYTHM

(Or, why your page is a filthy stinking liar)

The most deceitful character you'll encounter as a copywriter is easy to spot. He is thin, white and rectangular.

And, before you go rushing about confronting every pale and blockish person in your office, I should probably say I'm talking about the page.

You see, when you're writing - or rather evaluating what you've written - the words on the page can give you a false sense of achievement. Judge your writing only by the shape and structure of what you see and you could easily send something out into the world that glides on the eye and clangs in the brain.

In Stephen Fox's classic exploration of advertising, The Mirror Makers, he talks about copywriters learning 'to write for the ear'. In Fox's day this was due to the emergence of radio advertising as the dominant form, and he describes how 'simple, conversational language, repetitive and over punctuated, with short sentences and few pronouns' was the most effective way to arrest and engage a listener.

So rigorous was the craft of writing for the ear that writers would even restrict their use of s, f and m sounds, as they were harder for the listener to make out.

And, although radio is just one of many mediums for our words these days, what Fox describes is a fundamental principle of everything you write - rhythm.

It's so completely, unconditionally essential for you to read aloud the copy you've written, I'm not even going to strain your eyes by telling you to do it. If you don't, you are playing Russian roulette with the alphabet and are likely to find a harsh and pointy consonant embedded in your temple.

Instead I want to try and explain why it's such an important thing to do, and how much better it will make the lines you write.

Ursula K LeGuin, who is one of the finest writers about writing there's ever been, has this to say about the rhythm of words:

'The sound of language is where it all begins. The test of a sentence is 'does it sound right?' The basic elements of language are physical: the noise words make, the sounds and silences that make the rhythms, marking their relationship. Both the meaning and the beauty of the writing depend on these sounds and rhythms'.

Another excellent writer on the craft of writing, Eudora Welty, describes the intertwining of printed word with sound: 'ever since I was first read to, then started reading to myself, there has never been a line read that I didn't hear. As my eyes followed the sentence, a voice was saying it silently to me.'

But, without Welty's internal speaker system, no matter how diligently you glare at the page, there is no way for you to feel this sense of sound, silence and rhythm until you speak it aloud.

That's why, as well as reading out your copy as you're writing, you have to insist on reading it out loud when you present it – every time it's presented. Call me prim, but I'm not sure anyone will do a better job of performing a line than the person who has not only written the words, but crafted its delivery.

The reason all of this matters is simple. Flowing, rhythmic writing is more pleasurable to read and therefore more likely to be read and remembered.

Listen to pretty much any song by Jake Thackray and I guarantee you'll find it almost impossible to stop. You'll be hypnotised by the effortless rhythm of his lyrics, in the same way you can mentally incapacitate a shark by turning it upside down. Sort of.

Your writing should be aiming to achieve the same thing, slipping unobstructed into your readers' consciousness, smooth as a lubed eel.

The simplest way to achieve this in your writing is through careful and clever repetition. However, brace yourself for some puzzling resistance.

The origins of these objections can be traced back to some rigid and irrelevant lessons you were taught in English class. Benjamin Blatt, in his excellent book on creativity, 'Nabakov's Favourite Word is Mauve', talks about a teacher who told him never to start consecutive sentences with the same word, a technique known as anaphora.

Similarly, I once had a client tell me that 'good' copywriting should never repeat the same word twice within an ad. To get around this I simply flipped this young man upside down and tickled his belly.

Skim through the archives of the greatest ads ever written and you'll see quickly that this is nonsense. Repetition is a powerful way to not only build rhythm but to create something entirely memorable

Yes, it has to be handled with restraint and purpose. In The King's English, by Kingsley Amis (see what he did there?) he writes 'unintentional repetition is the most pernicious of errors. There could be no clearer sign of a writer who is incompetent, lazy, hurried, preoccupied, demoralised... Like other kinds of fault, this one is more readily detected by reading a passage aloud'. He's right. Repeating with purpose and as part of the creative construct is good. Repeating clumsily and by accident is unforgivable.

But if the alternative is dragging unwieldy and inappropriate words from the thesaurus every sentence, then it's clear that repetition is a risk worth taking.

(Blatt, by the way, smartly undermines his teacher's fallacy by pointing out that Kurt Vonnegut uses the phrase 'so it goes' 106 times in Slaughterhouse Five - accounting for 2.5% of all the words in the novel and not exactly hindering its success.)

Of course, I know that reading your words out loud can be daunting. In a career of reading my words out loud I've faced everything from embarrassed tittering to the face you'd make if you'd just seen a seagull vomit on a baby. But rhythm, as well as apparently being a dancer, is also the difference between your words falling off a cliff, or zip-wiring straight to their intended target.

Copywriting is

RESPONSIBILITY

(Or, why we need to take care of our words)

If there's one thing more appalling than someone who *loves* their job, it's someone who thinks their job makes a positive difference to the world.

Copywriters, you'll be disgusted to learn, often fall into both of these camps, earning them the distinction of being one of the few professions that almost perfectly divides their immediate world into people who don't understand what they do and people who don't want to hear about it.

Unsurprisingly, your author is very much one of those frightful hogs who believes copywriting 'can' (if not always 'does') nudge humanity into fulfilling and uplifting choices.

The obvious, and perfectly understandable, counter-argument to this is that we sell unwanted items to the credulous, and propagate a dreary culture of 'stuff'. There's no real defence to this – our professional existence is defined by our capacity to persuade, and most often that act of persuasion is to substitute 'want' for 'need' in the minds of people who could almost certainly be spending their money in better ways.

But, the very fact that our words not only seed desire but drive action confirms that the copywriter has the capacity, if not the occasion, to make the world a more pleasant experience.

Now, I'm not (quite) self-indulgent enough to pretend I can persuade anyone that copywriting is a medium for universal altruism, in 500 words. But I do feel like copywriters find themselves under a familiar, but far more pronounced, social obligation.

Without wishing to sound too shrill, the later years of the 2010s was a time where words got kicked in the balls.

Language has always been used to evade, diminish and antagonise, but recently we've seen precious words used with the very worst intentions.

Newspaper headlines, social media discourse and, yes, even our own sacred parish have all (perhaps with the best intentions, perhaps not) used language to frighten and divide.

George Orwell has been asking us to be angrier at obfuscation, or at least warier of the abuse of language, for a long time. In his essay, Politics and The English Language, he says:

'The great enemy of clear language is insincerity. When there is a gap between one's real and one's declared aims one turns, as it were, instinctively to long words and exhausted idioms, like a cuttlefish spurting out ink.'

Seeing this ink-cloud spread, anyone with a professional investment in the power of words is likely to have winced their way through years of froth, fury and fat-fingered tweet storms.

Even from a purely selfish point of view, it is bad business for any copywriter to witness the erosion of trust in the things we read.

But, rather than toss my Scrabble tile coffee mug on the bonfire of presidential vanities, I feel like we, one of modern life's weedier vocations, have been presented with the opportunity to fight.

David Hieatt wrote that people in the brand business should begin by 'defining their enemy.' I would urge copywriters young and old to do precisely the same.

And, unequivocally, our enemy is the misuse of language. I'm not talking about pedantry or sniggering at clumsy lines, I'm talking about the fundamental preservation of a word's value.

I doubt this should manifest itself in thousands of be-cardiganed copywriters storming Twitter HQ, armed with immaculately apostrophised placards.

Rather, it is a matter of us holding ourselves, our agencies, our peers and our clients to higher standards when it comes to defending the integrity of the alphabet. Copywriters are, as we know, exquisite liars, but it's for this very reason that we bear such a unique responsibility for the truth.

We have no control over what idiots say or what idiots believe, but we have a larger-than-average say in whether the printed page becomes a battleground or a playground.

RESPONSIBILITY

Copywriting is

BIG WORDS

(Or, size sometimes matters)

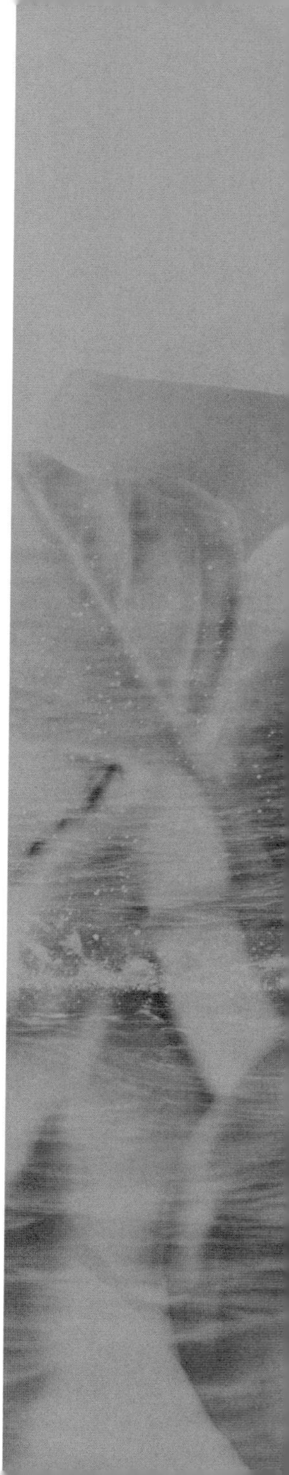

Ernest Hemingway being, amongst other things, a *prickly* old sod, is always good for a bruising literary retort.

For example, when William Faulkner got mildly sniffy about the simplicity – and implied lack of ambition – in Hemingway's famously sparse prose, Hemingway eloquently peeled a length of vital tissue off, what he saw as, his rival's sesquipedalian leanings.

'Poor Faulkner,' seethed Hem. 'Does he really think big emotions come from big words? He thinks I don't know the ten-dollar words. I know them all right. But there are older and simpler and better words, and those are the ones I use.'

The bare beauty of Hemingway's writing has seen him adopted as something of an inter-disciplinary mascot for modern copywriters. Here is an author who is, quite rightly, regarded as one of the most evocative voices of his, or any other, literary generation, and he achieved this without forking out for very many of the ten-dollar words.

I count myself very much amongst the copywriters who see Hemingway as a champion for extracting the most meaning from the fewest letters. You will perhaps struggle to find a copywriter who believes the 'older and simpler and better words' of Hemingway's writing are anything other than the foundation for how we should, and must, write.

And yet, safe in the knowledge that the great old bear of modern literature is unlikely to come after me with his many murderous implements, I do reserve a smidgeon of sympathy for Faulkner.

From a copywriting point of view, writing with the Hemingway technique – or at least the common understanding of it – will almost certainly produce better ads than mimicking a writer who sacrifices immediacy and familiarity for something longer, prettier and not especially more useful.

But there is a danger that copywriters have, as is our way, dogmatised the Hemingway position to the point of obstinacy and self-enforced austerity.

We, as a species, have a habit of building a cage around our own process and – worse – rationalising our restrictions, even when a better solution peeps through the bars.

In other words, too many copywriters have taught themselves to despise long words.

There is an exercise drummed into many of us that demands us to replace every word we write with something shorter, simpler and more familiar. And this is excellent advice – providing we retain the ability to discern when longer, stranger and more surprising words can add value to what we are trying to say.

An advert I saw recently for Ted Baker glasses read: 'Quite the Spectacle'. It stopped me in my tracks, partly because I am an irredeemable pervert for such things, and partly because it was the longest and most out-of-place word I had seen in an ad for a long time.

Under the Hemingway law of writing – not that he ever himself urged such a practice – we would spend far longer trying to substitute the word 'spectacle' for a more ordinary cousin, and in doing so strip out the personality and persuasiveness of the line.

I am being glib. I doubt any writer could be so beholden to a theory as to butcher an impressive line in the interests of compliance to a dead and disinterested novelist.

But I do believe that a great many of us would rule out presenting such a line purely because it clambers over the borders we have imposed on our own alphabetical territory.

Long words, funny-looking words, complex words and words valued at ten dollars and above, all have something to offer a copywriter – providing the moment, the audience, the challenge and the idea allow for it.

No copywriter could possibly craft a compelling message only from words of four syllables or above. But, using one or more to create drama, or surprise, or an unexpected shape, or even just to land a simple joke about glasses that look rather nice, is ten dollars well spent.

B

Copywriting is

ORIGINALITY

(Or, saying the things that haven't been said a million times before)

In a short story by Wells Tower, one of the characters describes himself as 'a bumblebee trying to fuck a marble.'

Give yourself the next forty years trawling through the complete human history of creative writing and I'm fairly confident you will *never* find a similar phrase.

Copywriting is ***Originality.***
(Or, saying the things that haven't been said a million times before)

An original use of words is what distinguishes any form of creative writing – our own included – from the ordinary, everyday writing we bang out without care. Unfortunately, a mere 2 million years into the history of the written word, you might find that a great deal of clever and surprising things have already been done.

Luckily, words are as close to an infinite resource as you're likely to find on this planet. The trick in writing something original is in knowing where to look for it.

The hardest and most unhelpful place to begin is under the misapprehension that today's originality can only ever be deep or complex. Gertrude Stein, a writer who knew more than most about the power of difference, wrote of her character (who also happened to be herself), 'she always says she dislikes the abnormal, it is so obvious. She says the normal is so much more simply complicated and interesting.'

This is so true it would not be the worst idea you've ever had for a tattoo. The simple, the familiar and the everyday are potent stores of imaginative potential. It's just a matter of seeing the thing we see all the time in the way we never have before.

Original expression is, after all, the only way for us to perceive new meaning in the world. In Language in Danger, Andrew Dalby writes 'It is difficult to imagine that we could have made the progress we have made in investigating the world and understanding one another without, sometimes, saying things that no one had ever said before'.

It's a principle that takes you all the way back to Edward de Bono and his book 'The Use of Lateral Thinking' – a genuinely essential examination of what happens when we stop allowing logic to make our choices for us.

De Bono says 'it is not possible to dig a hole in a different place by digging the same hole deeper'. A copywriter's translation would be that it is not possible to change someone's mind if we make the same argument, only louder.

Originality in copywriting is, above all, about a devotion to language. It is about believing in it wholeheartedly and protecting it from misuse. In his book 'On Tyranny' Timothy Snyder urges us to 'avoid pronouncing the phrases everyone else does. Think up your own way of speaking, even if only to convey that thing you think everyone else is saying'.

We have a responsibility to do that as human beings who have the capacity to write and speak. That responsibility is dramatically multiplied when you are in the business of using words to affect the way people think and act.

Originality, like creativity itself, is one of those essential – but frustratingly intangible – qualities that is impossible for a copywriter to either control or dispose of.

David Bohm, in an utterly compelling book called 'On Creativity' suggests that 'one prerequisite for originality is clearly that a person shall not be inclined to impose his preconceptions on the fact as he sees it. Rather he must be able to learn something new, even if that means that the ideas and notions that are comfortable or dear to him may be overturned'.

Comfort and dearness, in terms of creative thinking and innovative writing, are like trying to paddle a canoe with a weasel instead of any oar. We must let go of everything we love, understand and believe to be true and try to make sense of a problem as if we've never seen or heard of it in our lives.

There are no shortcuts to transforming yourself into a vessel for original thoughts and expressions. But there are methods you can start to force into your own everyday process – with and without the pencil – that can help you become a far more vigilant guardian against assumption, generalisation and mindless conformity.

Mike Sharples, author of How We Write: Writing as Creative Design, says that 'composing, then, is a process not of emptying the mind, but of actively reconstructing it... A writer in the act of composing is in a continual mental tension between interpreting existing ideas and creating new ones.'

The trick every copywriter must therefore learn is knowing when the words on your page are old ideas – and what you can do to transform them into something new.

Copywriting is

MEANING

(Or, this isn't a beauty contest)

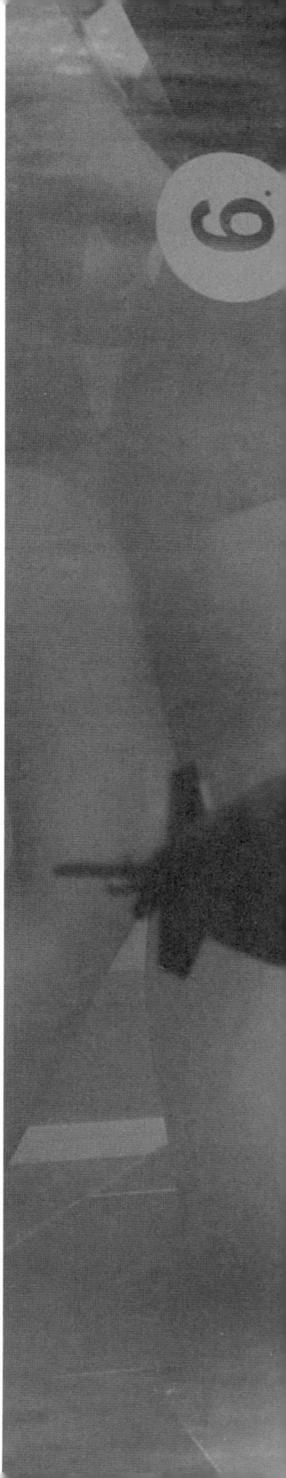

Like a telephone made
from ice cream or
a velvet submarine,
copywriting that
is beautiful but
meaningless is not
actually copywriting.

In How We Write: Writing as Creative design, Mike Sharples says 'a message is a message not because it is written in words on paper or etched in gold, but because it forms a conceptual link between different minds'. And it is that link, that fundamental connection between suggestor and receiver that will define the quality and the effectiveness of your copy far more than the elegance of your phrasing.

Too often, especially in a copywriter's own judgment, the glorious line that carries no meaning is valued higher than the effective one expressed in an ordinary way.

This does not have to be an 'either/or' decision – we could, should, must be aiming to achieve both.

Raymond Williams writes that 'the advertiser is working directly on images and dreams' – not in the sense that we create something stunning without substance, but through the careful implanting of new desires, unexpressed need and a primal will to live better than we do right now.

What a copywriter needs to appreciate is that they alone are not responsible for the meaning taken away from the words they write. There is another party who has a say in how our words are received and utilised. The person we are addressing with those words.

There's an oft-quoted (overly oft in some people's opinion) Hemingwayism about the reader bringing more to the page than the writer intended. And that is one of the strange truths that a copywriter must bear in mind even though they have limited influence over how this actually unfolds.

W Somerset Maugham, another fellow who could make words dance like flamingos on a hen night, said 'each of us has his little communication to make, a restricted one, and from all these communications readers can choose, according to their own inclinations, what suits them'.

Maugham had literature in mind, but the same observation works in our world just as well. The words that an audience reads cease to be yours the second they enter the reader's brain. From then on, they bare only a trace of your hand and are instead the property and plaything of someone else's mind – subject to inspection and dissection, action and rejection.

As copywriters, we can't worry too much about what happens to our words once they enter the heads of our audience – but equally, we cannot assume our part of the job has been done and done well.

'Marketing has been about allowing a product or service to confer meaning on the purchaser. Even our take-out coffee container is a signifier of meaning and belonging' writes Alex Evans in the Myth Gap – reminding us that the copywriters' job is to plant the seeds of what this brand, product or service may say about the people who choose it.

Writing with meaning is often misinterpreted as an opportunity to glorify the brand rather than donate that reflected glory to your customers. Bernadette Jiwa, in as pithy a maxim as we're likely to see, says: 'your customers don't want to know what you do. They want to know how you're going to enable them to do what they want to do'.

By reserving meaning for the people who read the ad rather than squandering it all on the people who paid for it, you can elevate your copy from elegantly immemorable to persuasively beautiful.

It is impossible to pluck the relevant meaning from our own minds, just as it is impossible to guess a person's age by examining their kettle. The only way to find the meaning your copy demands is to know precisely the meaning your audience will look for – which in turn means knowing precisely what meaning meaningfully means in their world.

Ignore, forget or lose the meaning in your copy and your words will be hollow, blown eggs still expected to make omelettes for the breakfast rush.

Philip Collins (not that one) is a political speechwriter who also wrote an extraordinary book on that craft. In it, he points out that 'the cause of the distance between the people and politics is empty talk'. The same distance exists between people and advertising, thanks to adverts that bear glitter on the outside and carry nothing within. And, in a business defined more meaningfully by results than creation, there is nothing scarier than staring across this particular distance, wondering if you'll ever reach the other side.

Copywriting is

ALIVE

(Or, death to zombie words)

As *anyone* who has ever binged heartily on 'The Walking Dead' knows, there can be some pretty powerful residual effects.

Most worrying amongst these is a disturbing urge to smash slow moving pedestrians in the head with a shovel.

Less potentially convictable is a tendency to view aspects of your own life through the weary eyes of the shovel-wielders in the show. More specifically, twisted by an over-indulgence in the slobber and gore of a TV show, you begin to examine your own world as if the zombie apocalypse were just meandering around the corner.

Only for me, inescapably tethered to the alphabet like a sacrificial goat, the zombies I began to recognise in my own world were not drooling noisily at the window but were in fact on the page.

Zombie words are those that used to be full of life and purpose and now, struck down by a strange and virulent disease, are dead. Or at least, un-dead, dragging their inanimate forms around the page with all the verve of a recently smashed moth.

The infection, in this instance, is less about having your ankle munched by a frothing, dead-eyed paperboy but rather stems from simple over-use.

Amongst the droning, plodding victims of this contagion are words you probably use in your copy every day – often not staring at them closely enough to notice that flesh is oozing from their bones like a Malteser in a bulky man's armpit.

Words like 'Amazing', 'Genuine' and 'Discover' are the most frequent and formidable victims. Where once they could communicate awe, authenticity and adventure respectively, now they squat dimly amongst your copy in a pool of their own drool and decay.

Worse still, like true zombies they gnaw mindlessly at the life around them – dragging strong and vital copy down to their own flaccid, fetid level.

Zombie words are a common toxin in modern copywriting. Trapped in our own habits and comforts, copywriters often don't notice when a word that used to mean something now feels tired and implausible.

We should conduct zombie sweeps at regular intervals – combing through our copy to make sure that dead words aren't spreading their malaise amongst the living.

And of course, when you track down these zombie words, there's only one proper course of action. And that's a shovelling...

Copywriting is

CONTROL

(Or, why letting go is the best way of holding on)

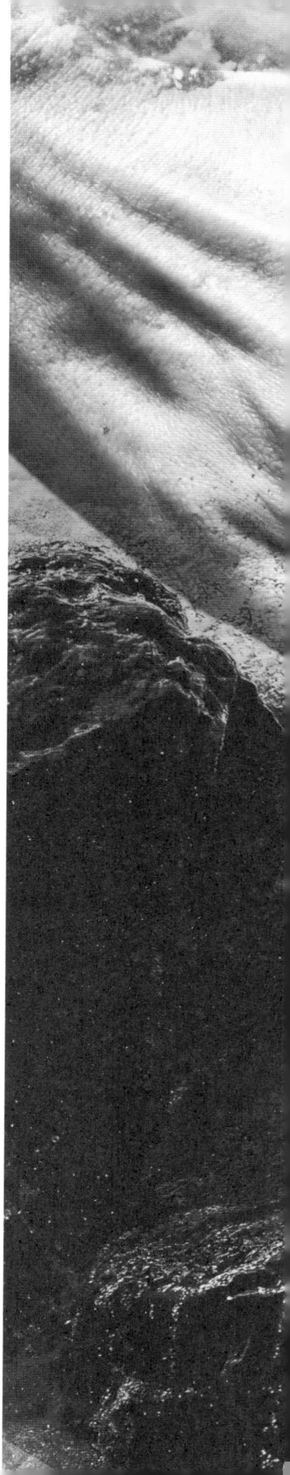

The best way to illustrate what this section is about, rather than with my own half-baked words, is through this amazing passage from *The Writing Life* by Annie Dillard:

A work in progress quickly becomes feral.

It reverts to a wild state overnight.

It is barely domesticated, a mustang, one which you one day fastened to a halter, but which now you cannot catch.

It is a lion you cage in your study.

As the work grows, it gets harder to control; it is a lion growing in strength.

You must visit it every day and reassert your mastery over it.

If you skip a day you are, quite rightly, afraid to open the door to its room.

You enter its room with bravura, holding a chair at the thing and shouting 'Simba!'

As well as being a rather wonderful example of someone in control of their words, it's the perfect description of a copywriter's plight.

One of the most barbarous assumptions in our business is that 'anyone can write'. Even if this were within the gravitational orbit of truth, it fails to account for the fact that the writing we do is very different from the day-to-day mashing together of familiar words.

Words, in our field, are exactly as Dillard describes them: wild, hostile and untethered.

Without proper care and application, the words on your page will squirm like a hooked eel. Without a forceful grip on your pen, you are merely a conduit for hieroglyphs rather than a ringmaster for meaning.

Asserting this mastery over words is what separates the copywriters from Gary who's good for a funny limerick in a birthday card.

But, if words are such ferocious and disobedient creatures, how are we supposed to bend them to our will?

The secret to policing your own page is both simple and horribly complex. We could, for example, rigidly impose a structure, plot a direction and fixate on an outcome.

But good copywriting is a fluid, emotional craft and, at the risk of sounding wanky, it is a product of following your instincts rather than the rule book.

However, this is precisely the sort of control every copywriter must learn to impose. Think of it less like piloting a boat across a pond and more like clinging to a log in a surging river.

Words can be steered, even as they tumble out of you, but sometimes it's better to submit to the diversions they want to take.

A massively undervalued tool in controlled copywriting is the ability to, as they say, knock it on the head. Scratching it out, screwing it up, tapping out a tasty beat on the delete key - all of these things will reassert your stewardship of where your writing needs to go.

If you get too precious or protective of a route, you become its passenger. Sometimes, the most creatively optimistic thing you can do is hop off the log and watch from the shallows as it topples over the falls or clatters face first into a leaping salmon.

Assuming that control means never loosening your grip will get you to the end of your copy, but it will muffle the growl your writing should have had. Equally only allowing yourself to deal in certainties as your write, rather than allowing strange looking words to ferment into something intoxicating, holds you back. Certainty, as the artist Grayson Perry observes, is a dodgy business.

It's not easy to find that balance between trusting the direction of your words while shepherding them. But the more you can learn to decipher the thrusts and tugs and meanderings of the way your mind wants to write, the better you are at taming the process, without domesticating the results.

CONTROL

Copywriting is

DANGER

(Or, the perils of certainty)

Of all the *sinister* forces that will try and trip you up as a copywriter, none succeed more fully in tearing a hole in the knee of your cords than believing you've got it right.

In his wonderful book Simplexity, Jeffery Kluger points out that 'the marketing landscape is littered with the remains of ideas that once seemed like sure hits until customers got a good look at them and closed their wallets.'

Far worse than a mere fallacy, a sense of certainty is often the hallmark of truly thoughtless creative. Who, for example, amongst the many well-paid people who gleefully approved that notorious Kendall Jenner Pepsi ad, did so with anything less than fulsome and fervent certainty?

If your copy is aiming towards certainty you may as well be pinging tennis balls at the moon. And yet, in an industry that increasingly overestimates its own omniscience, you may often find that certainty isn't merely the aim, but the expectation.

It's difficult for lowly pencil jockeys such as ourselves to dissuade our betters of their data-based fanaticism. But we should at least try.

How we do this is by refusing to shackle ourselves to some apocryphal concept of surety. Let the planners and the chiefs and the big cheeses grow complacent in their false assurances, and instead write something dangerous.

Dangerous in the sense that any truly death-defying feat does not allow for the possibility of a stumble. Or rather, it allows only for the possibility of one, very long, very final stumble.

Copywriting should not follow the path, but scale the cliff. It may take more time and you may accumulate more bruises, but that's the price for forging a route rather than following one. Just as in one of those wildly overused motivational internet quotes – that may or may not belong to William Faulkner – we are told 'you cannot swim for new horizons until you have the courage to lose sight of the shore.'

William Hazlitt says that 'danger is a good teacher, and makes apt scholars' and that is precisely why free-climbing as a copywriter, however perilous, makes you more accomplished. Hazlitt also notes that disgrace, defeat and exposure to immediate scorn or laughter are equally good at strengthening the resolve and eroding the sensitivities that get in the way of your best work.

By taking the dangerous trail you are most unlikely to arrive at the familiar, the presumptuous or the expected solution. You may not arrive immediately at the best answer, but at least you will be further away from the safe, and therefore forgettable, territory.

I'm not saying there's no place for rational thinking in your copywriting, just a recognition that this part of your brain has a chemical reticence when it comes to the unfamiliar. Jonah Lerner, in The Decisive Moment, observes that 'when the rational brain hijacks the mind, people tend to make all sorts of decision-making mistakes... they ignore the wisdom of their emotions'. For Lerner, this means us blindly trusting the ideas that sound right, rather those that feel right.

Emotion, often dismissed as the indefinably fluffy whim of the creative, is what we are writing toward. The people who see the ad you write may make a rational choice, but that rational choice will be triggered, underpinned or reinforced by an emotional response.

We can't make everyone around us trust in the virtue of the unpredictable. All we can do is prove that a bit of dangerous thinking is a rewarding risk to take.

DANGE R

Copywriting is

TALKING

(Or, why good words die in dry mouths)

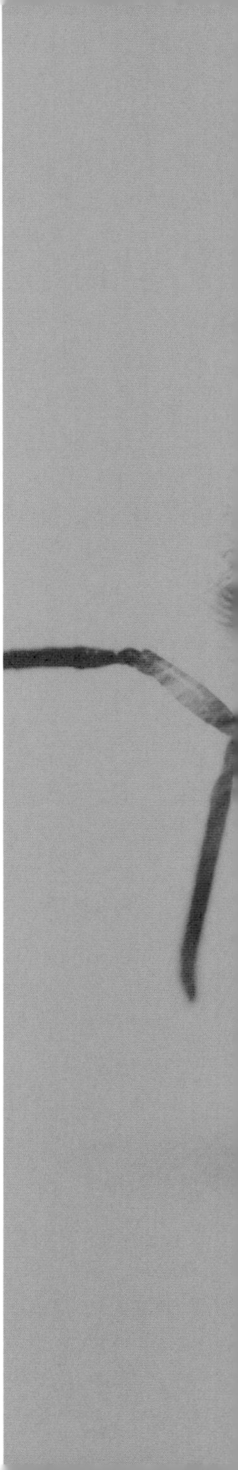

Imagine, dear reader, that you were a *zookeeper*. Imagine you excelled in every aspect of zookeepery, from expert foliage distribution to legendary iguana management.

Now imagine, for all your magnificence in zoo coordination, you scream like a gazelle and sweat pure liquid meat the second you step into the wolf enclosure.

In other words, no matter how excellent you are at one half of your job, it's your shortcomings in the second half that will define your career.

Now, unless you suffer from a rare case of metaphor blindness, you can probably see where this is going.

In copywriting, there is a part of the job that doesn't require you to write or think or even deal confidently with commas. It requires you to speak.

You may have been in presentations where a client has graciously volunteered to read your copy from the page while you gaze out of the window in mute contemplation. But mostly we are expected to read aloud what we have written.

And here is the problem. Many of us feel safest, smartest and most invincible when dealing with words on a page. But, as it is with anyone who expresses themselves best in writing, being asked to read those words out loud - to actual people - can easily strip off our sense of invincility.

I have no idea why this is, although you could argue there is a certain pressure attached to verbalising something you know works so well on paper. As Nick Cave says 'there are two parts to being a songwriter – writing the songs and sending them out into the world. Sending them into the world is the terrifying part.'

Naturally, this doesn't apply to every copywriter, and I have seen writers liquify a room with the assuredness of their delivery.

Like most things in our business, Don Draper is to blame. There is an expectation, on both sides, that we do not merely articulate what we have written, but dramatise it. And while there are many reasons you and I got into copywriting - the sex, the glory, the knitwear - I doubt many of us signed up for the performance.

Unfortunately, no matter how ferociously your bowels may rumble at the prospect of 'a reading', it is an essential part of the role.

Call me proprietorial (or just plain ball-greedy) but I believe that no one can do a better job of 'selling in' the copy than the copywriter.

Equally, I've been to enough presentations where stunning writing has been dismissed because the delivery only managed to strangle and subdue its merits.

As we agreed in an earlier chapter, we should all be reading our copy out loud anyway, unless of course we're blessed with a rare, internal calculator for rhythm. (Hint: no one has this.)

But it's a different beast when we're reading it to the people paying (big/good/adequate) money for our ability as a writer.

So what do we do? Hire actors who have played minor villains in The Bill? Fake a serious bee sting seconds before it's our turn to talk?

Here's the twist. I have no advice. And even if I did, no one can tell you how to best train your voice to do justice to your words.

But whatever your method for making your copy do to the ear what it does to the eye, we all need to put our mouth where the money is.

Otherwise all we are is bones in a wolf's belly.

"TALKING"

Copywriting is

MADNESS

(Or, prepare to be obsessed)

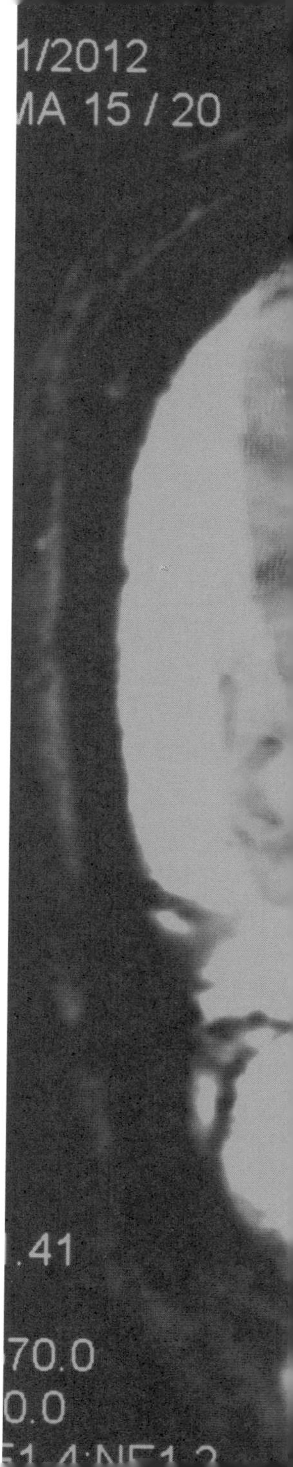

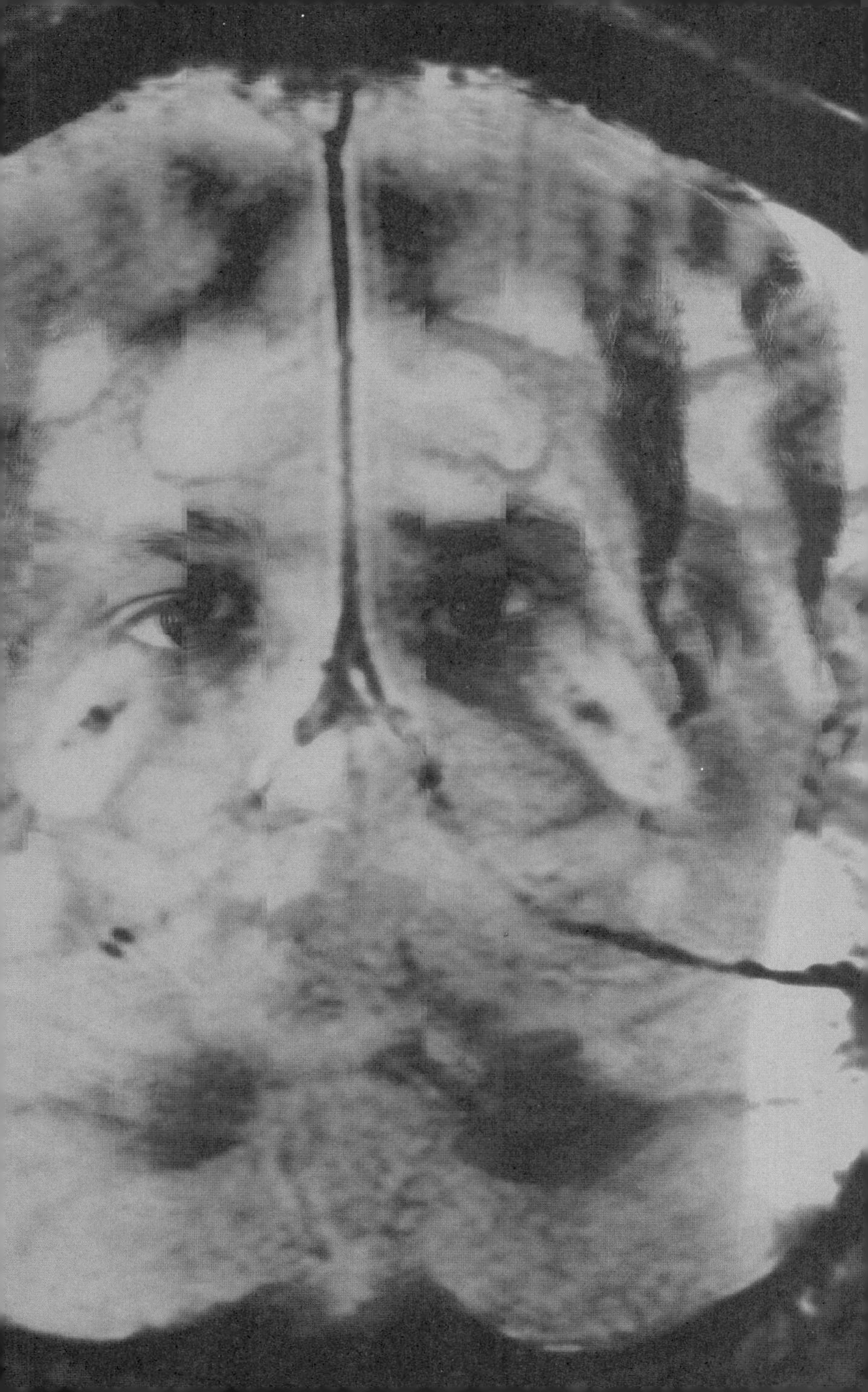

Poking around the mind of anyone in this peculiar crocodile-wrestle we call advertising is a good way to see some strange and terrible things. So, to jab a finger into the wasp nest that is your own professional psyche is less the subject of a whimsical book and more the act of a dangerous lunatic.

Nevertheless, the psychological arrangement of the common copywriter contains the kind of conflict, delusion and outright mania that compels us to peel away the tin foil helmet and expose the gibbering truth. (I'll warn you though, this chapter contains a dangerous amount of wild generalisation.)

In many copywriters there exists a peculiar sense of entitlement. Not that we demand a dressing room filled with expensive pencils and precisely chilled Vimto, but more a requirement to be listened to.

The very nature of the job is to be, not the loudest voice, but the most compelling – to say something conventional and familiar in a way that feels extraordinary and unavoidable. How often have you seen a copywriter deflated by a message that, within the creative maelstrom, whimpers meekly to be noticed?

We're also guilty of a simmering indignation, a righteous contempt for those who believe that anyone with fingers, eyes and access to ink is capable of copywriting. And we see these characters everywhere, even lurking in the shadows of our best and most productive client relationships.

A feeling that our contribution isn't quite as valued by some as we know it should be is perhaps the fuel for another common anxiety – a crippling, obsessive, maddening perfectionism.

Leave some copywriters alone with a perfectly constructed headline and they will tear it apart, showering the walls with a splatter of increasingly unsatisfying synonyms. I've known many a copywriter hunt down a final draft on its way out of the door, paralysed by a dread that there may be too many, or indeed not enough, commas.

Your classic, corn-fed copywriter is also unsettlingly comfortable with their own professional schizophrenia. We are characters with dozens of voices and perspectives rattling around in our heads, with the ability to argue for and against any particular point with equal conviction.

And yet, while we're capable of cultivating all kinds of disparate voices, we never truly let go of our own. Even in that 600-word manual for a rotary lawnmower, our own unique style murmurs quietly around the grassy edges.

We are, I suppose, beasts of imagination tethered inescapably to reality. We define success by creative brilliance, knowing ultimately it is only properly defined by commercial performance. And amongst all this, we yo-yo in and out of an odd state of immersion – rapt by a brief about bacon, or shoes or cat blankets all the time knowing that none of it really exists. Copywriting, like advertising, is the art of sculpting fog.

At the heart of this is the unusual evolution of creativity itself. As Alex Osborn points out in Wake Up Your Mind, creative thinking for our ancestors was not merely an interesting way to pay for new cardigans, it was what kept them alive. 'Sheer necessity forced our forefathers to think up new and better ways of doing things' writes Osborn. 'To keep alive, they had to work their ingenuity overtime. Our softer living numbs our sense of enterprise and deadens our creative spirit'. We are the exception, still living rather softly but also still dependent on imagination as the measure of our value to the tribe.

And that's just a few of the neuroses and peculiarities I can recognise in myself and copywriters I've known well. There are some of us who share these, just as there are some with no recognition at all for this slightly shambling portrait of our profession. There are some, I'm quite sure, with an even more complex relationship with the work.

Whether it's the fundamental strangeness of the job that sends us this way, or whether it's our inherent idiosyncrasies that navigate us to this outlandish working life, I'm not sure.

Ink on the page, ink on our fingers and, without doubt, ink on the brain.

MADNESS

Copywriting is

CRITICISM

(Or, why feedback is a better gift than a bike)

THIS WAY UP

There are very few character flaws that will *prevent* you from succeeding in a creative career. In fact, a great many of those deficiencies will be precisely why you do succeed.

But there is one particular characteristic that no professional creative can possibly be without. And that is to do with their relationship with feedback.

Colour-blind designers, copywriters with a disregard for apostrophes and creative thinkers with a restricted imagination can all cheat, disguise or otherwise soften their failings. But, if you are unable to accept and administer challenge you will find a creative life to be a miserable and perpetually hostile existence.

A creative director I know, who cheerfully recounts the stories of bruising and belittling presentations to her superiors, once said to me that feedback is the breakfast of champions.

And, while she is entirely right, the chemical and evolutionary make-up of our brains is determined to stand in the way of such valuable wisdom.

The human brain's natural response to criticism or contradiction is one of fear and self-defence. It sees criticism as an almost primal threat – reasoning, from the shadows of its caveman past, that being wrong is an excellent way to get yourself gobbled up by a mammoth or accidentally set up home in a barely dormant volcano.

Anyone entering the business of paid creativity has to be able to strangle the instinct to flee from, or fight against, criticism – partly because it will be too exhausting to spend your whole career in this manic state of preservation, partly because feedback is pretty much the only gift of value this industry can provide.

The author and journalist Kathryn Schulz, in her book Being Wrong: Adventures in the Margin of Error says 'being wrong is hard and humbling and sometimes even dangerous. But in the end it is a journey and a story'. In other, less good, words being wrong provides you with drama and peril and decisions that need taking. Being right provides you with, aside from smugness or relief (depending on your personality), precisely nothing.

Feedback, the giving and taking of, is one of those industry obsessions that compel us to seek out – and then rather manhandle – evidence and understanding from the scientific world.

A study that, a few years ago, seemed to be everywhere in creative circles was by Dr Carla Jefferies who, in my inadequate simplification, suggested that a failure to give constructive feedback is more about protecting ourselves than the people whose work we are commenting upon.

It then becomes a cycle of withholding, a pattern of silent abuse where none of us learn and none of grow because none of us are prepared to say there is a better way to do what we're doing.

The idea of 'killing your darlings' is something that every creative will encounter, hopefully, in the formative years of their creativity. But what few of us are taught is that it's just as important to kill our bias. Our bias, our understanding of the way the world is and should be, makes it impossible for us to listen to – or indeed respect – anyone who sees things differently.

With this sort of mindset – what the psychologists would call 'fixed' as opposed to 'growth' – we end up holding a stick that offers nothing but shitty ends. You still have to hear criticism, but you are unable or unwilling to learn from it. It's a little like a climber tumbling off a cliff, breaking their leg and still not having learned to tie a more secure knot for next time.

The fundamental misinterpretation – and perhaps misrepresentation – of criticism in creative practice is that it is somehow about power. It is not, or at least, it should never be that.

Feedback should be about generosity – the generosity of observation, challenge and suggestion that can make your idea better. Seen in these terms, and not as a platform for dissolving your confidence or demeaning your efforts, feedback becomes something to be treasured.

Perhaps because criticism has often been adopted as a tool for vendettas and one-upmanship, it has earned a reputation for savagery and demolition. A famous criticism often, but not accurately, attributed to the humourist Ambrose Bierce was that 'the covers of this book are too far apart'. A witty put-down, undoubtedly, but this branch of weaponised feedback is not criticism in a true or meaningful sense.

Instead, consider this thought from transcendental philosopher, and all-round serious sausage, Ralph Waldo Emerson, who wrote in his journal: 'Let me never fall into the vulgar mistake of dreaming that I am persecuted whenever I am contradicted.'

Criticism is not about you, your sensitivities, your upbringing, your art or your haircut – it is about the work. And, during the working day, these distinct continents of personality may have nothing at all to do with each other.

As you can see, the nature and purpose of criticism has preoccupied artists as much, if not a great deal more, than scientists.

One particular quotation, that was hastily superimposed onto an inspirational sunset, was from Will Self in a Guardian feature about writers and their relationship to, and experience of, failure.

Self said 'a creative life cannot be sustained by approval any more than it can be destroyed by criticism' and you can see why it was so heartily adopted by the creative community as, at best, a mantra and, at worst, an incantation against the meanies who don't like your words or pictures.

What is missing for me is the idea that a creative life can very much be sustained, and indeed propelled, by criticism – providing the receiver sees it for what it is and recognises how they may use it.

I much prefer an observation from the same article, from the writer Howard Jacobson. He says that 'art is made by those who consider themselves to have failed at whatever isn't art'.

Similarly, many people arrive in creative practice based on what could be called 'failures'. We, or at least our minds, have failed to follow an ordinary path. We have failed to conform to the idea that the world is fixed and cannot be manipulated into something better. We have failed, spectacularly and irretrievably, at being conventional.

We turn up to day one of our creative lives, perhaps unknowingly, as veterans in failure. If only we could bring the same degree of perspective and clarity to our creative failures – and use them as a way, the only way, to become better and braver at what we do.

CRITIcISM

Copywriting is

PAIN

(Or, If copywriting doesn't hurt, you're not doing it right)

Rust Cohle, the mumbling, shambling, preposterously attractive copper from True Detective says that ‘life’s barely long enough to get good at one thing... be careful what you get *good* at.’

And while Rust managed to get good at smouldering and mystical ramblings, most of us have decided to get good at copywriting. Which suggests that we, despite the warning, have not been at all careful.

From the outside, copywriting appears to be both a pristine temple of creative expression and an improbable way to pay your rent.

On the inside, at least in its darker moments, it can be demoralising, frustrating and the very antithesis of what a creative life looked like in your head.

Trot merrily into the copywriting life with your sensitivities on full display and you may find yourself gratefully pursuing that career in golf course maintenance your grandad always spoke so uninspiringly of.

But that's not to say that hardening yourself to the harsher realities of the job is a barrier to having a truly marvellous old time. In fact, I'd say such a thickening of the skin is imperative if you don't see yourself snapping pencils on your forehead and storming out of agencies every six weeks

Copywriting, though wonderful and prosperous and genuinely fulfilling, is also laced with pain. The trick is not to feel it.

Even if you've only dabbled so far in the copywriting life, even if your ink pot is more than half full and the glimmer of good fortune is yet to sustain its first chip, you will have noticed that something is very wrong with what we do.

We are, effectively, creative people at the whim of less creative people. We are the agile and wily convict who could break free from this chain gang if only we weren't cuffed to a timid and asthmatic embezzler of old ladies.

I'm being unkind. But, on the whole, the creativity we bring to the business must pass through several filters in which creativity is not always the main concern.

All it takes is one hesitant account manager, one worn-down creative director or one inflexible client to pull the wings off your idea and then ask you to fashion new ones. With a bigger logo.

And, if we're honest enough about the life we've chosen,

we can see both the reason for this and the impossibility of it changing.

This isn't a surrender. This isn't me advising you to roll over and let someone with a bigger office than you tickle the spark out of your weary tummy.

Instead it is an invitation to not merely embrace the pain, but to understand it. To learn that a wild and provocative idea cannot merely be smuggled past sceptical minds, but must be convincing beyond, or perhaps because of, that very wildness.

The Author, Georges Simenon once said 'I think that everyone who does not need to be a writer, who thinks he can do something else, ought to do something else'. Most of us may be able to do other things, but we also very much need to write.

And, rather than allowing that need to wither, we have little choice but to take ownership of the pain we're sure to face. That means writing bravely, and creating work that will win the arguments for you - arguments that are never settled simply in terms of beauty and imagination.

After all, it's already too late to get good at something else.

PAIN

Copywriting is

COMPLICATED

*(Or, the million things you can't control...
but must try to anyway)*

In what we may conservatively describe as one of the most *important* books on advertising ever written, The Theory and Practice of Advertising, psychologist Walter Dill Scott has this to say about how your audience may respond to ads that ask them to do something (oh, and please excuse the pronouns, this book was written in 1904):

'We are perfectly willing to obey as long as we are unconscious of the fact. But let anyone see that he has been commanded and his attitude is changed; he becomes obstinate instead of pliant.'

Even now, more than 100 years on, it is a thought so pertinent that it could easily be ascribed onto, say, a big red bus.

Ask anyone to outline what they fundamentally despise about advertising – and this may take a while – and the perception that you are being commanded often comes out higher than the suggestion you are being manipulated.

What Dill perfectly summarises is the strange relationships human beings have to their own sense of agency – most of the time oblivious to the hidden mechanics of choice except when you notice external forces at work and suddenly become as defiant as a boisterous dog with your best tea towel.

Dill also notes that 'it is but rarely that the ordinary person weighs all the evidence before he acts. After he has acted, he may think over the motives which might have prompted him, and may even deceive himself into thinking that he acted because he weighed the evidence, when, in fact, no such motives entered his mind at the time of action.'

What's more, that same stimulation of need and desire that may cause someone to act is itself liable to alter or even fizzle out altogether. As Alain de Botton writes in Status Anxiety: 'The quickest way to stop noticing something may be to buy it – just as the quickest way to stop appreciating a person may be to marry them'.

Which goes a long way to explaining why advertising is such a surprisingly complex and conflicted business to be in. Seen from this perspective, the creative bit suddenly seems like an absolute doddle – at least in comparison to the frothing contradictions and indignity of a human brain that doesn't know why it chose what it chose, but will furiously deny that it was persuaded by anything other than its own rational machinery.

Think of the big red Brexit bus (I know we're trying to forget it). If ever there was a manifestation of humanity's susceptibility for persuasion – and its abdication of critical scrutiny – it would be that slogan on that bus telling you something and knowing you will accept it for what it is.

In the wobbly-kneed beginnings of your creative advertising career you will often hear that we are in the business of winning attention. True enough, but simply claiming someone's passing glance or even earning a cursory scan of our message is not nearly enough to make our profession worthy of its existence.

Instead we are in the business of *purposeful attention* – getting noticed, of course, but then doing something meaningful with that attention.

And that is the spiky string of bones in your breakfast kipper – the part of the path on which we must tread very carefully, even though it is impossible to predict which is a stepping stone and which a sleeping crocodile.

Attention, now more than ever, is a finite resource. We do not have an infinite capacity for absorbing information or engaging with external stimuli.

Instead, our brains have unknowingly submitted a great deal of control to what Daniel Levitan, in The Organised Mind, describes as an 'attentional filter'. This, according to Levitan is the nightclub bouncer in our mind that determines what is, and what is not, worth telling the rest of the brain about. 'Due to the attentional filter' says Levitan 'we end up experiencing a great deal of the world on autopilot – not registering the complexities, nuances and often the beauty of what is right in front of us'.

Combine the two pieces of wisdom we've introduced in this chapter, from Dill and Levitan, and you start to see that the human brain is simultaneously capable of making irrational choices, ignoring our message entirely and defying anything they perceive as an urge to think or act which didn't unquestionably originate from within. Which leaves a degree of wriggle room that a common earthworm would describe as 'a bit pokey'.

So, now we know the multiple, overlapping and also wildly contradictory challenges of making a human brain act on your advert, what can we do about it?

Part of the answer lies in recognising that attention has a cost attached. It is finite, it is a compromise, it is a 'this' or 'that' exchange.

The key then is to make sure we are very much the 'this', rather than the 'that'. The ads we create and the messages we craft don't just have to earn attention, they have to do so by depriving something else of that same attention. And it's not as if the only thing we are competing with is other ads - we are competing with the entire world, other people, art, media, news, nature, conflict, emotion, the actual fucking sky.

It's a daunting job for something as relatively inconsequential as an advert to take on. It's even more so when we allow ourselves to recognise, despite the data and the science and the mountain of books that have tried to explain it, that human beings are simply unpredictable. 'It is quite difficult to detect any universal pattern at all' says Simon Blackburn in Think. 'Human beings can grow to make killing fields and they can grow to make gardens.'

But, if you at least understand the competition for human attention, in every sense *and* you understand the brain's ability to filter, rationalise and even resist our appeals *and* the ferocious unpredictability of which one it will decide to do, then at least you will have popped the asphyxiating bubble of creative for creative's sake.

Copywriting is

BELIEF

(Or, there's nothing embarrassing about a bad line)

If you have a person in your mind who represents complete and unfailing support for your creative efforts, you are *lucky*. If that person in your mind fills you with doubt and shame and a fear that what you are writing is wrong, poor or worthless – then you are normal.

Doubt is a democratic affliction – it has some hold over everyone who has ever attempted to create, regardless of how confident they may appear or how successful they have become.

This chapter does not allow for the possibility that you, as a creative or a copywriter, have never felt like a fraud – quite simply because I'm yet to meet someone in our profession who hasn't wrestled with these feelings on some level.

The first thing to say, then, is welcome to the Society for Imposters and Inadequates. Our order is burstingly full, but we never like to turn away a new member.

You will find an endless source of material on explaining or observing the nature of the inner-censor that lurks in creative people. I will be deeply surprised – and not a little suspicious – if you find something that claims to cure it.

The author, DBC Pierre describes our internal anti-fan club as 'a jury'. This jury has been installed in our minds 'to save us from being embarrassed or arrested'. It is often made up from the real people in our lives we are most afraid of disappointing, or at least being judged by.

Personally, I remember one teacher from school who behaved as if anyone attempting to think or act differently from his narrow view of ambition and virtue was, at best a fantasist, and at worst a deviant.

Even though I know that man is an idiot, he remains on my jury, arguing with the zeal of the pompous that I am getting it all wrong.

Pierre believes we should be doing the following: 'check who's on it and eliminate them for the purpose of writing. Write as if nobody will ever see the work. Make a pact never to reveal it. We have to write as if even we're not in the room'.

Of course, he isn't suggesting you should lock away every word you produce and never let them be seen by human eyes. It's tricky to be a copywriter if no one has ever read your copy.

Instead he is urging us to alter our mentality when it comes to writing. Postpone the judgement and simply write (see the chapter on 'Exploding').

Give your jury a bag of chewy fruits and ask them to go and play quietly on the A46 while you work. Stop trying to write and wonder if you're writing well all at the same time. You can only do one of those things to the fullest in any moment.

It's a trick that Lewis Hyde, in his examination of the creative spirit The Gift calls 'that phase of our work in which the artist lays evaluation aside so that the gift may come forward'.

Hyde goes on to illustrate his point with the thoughts of Beat poet Allen Ginsberg who explains not only the embarrassment of spontaneous creativity, but also it's unique value.

Hyde quotes Ginsberg as saying: 'the parts that embarrass you most are usually the most interesting poetically, are usually the most naked of all, the rarest, the goofiest, the strangest and most eccentric and at the same time the most representative, the most universal'. Protecting ourselves as we write from potential humiliation when our work is seen prevents us from writing with the recklessness and shamelessness that almost always produces the extraordinary idea.

Another important distinction we must make is between how a bad idea begins and how it ends up. In that most iconic of all advertising explorations, Hey Whipple Squeeze This, the authors urge us to 'embrace the suck'. They meant this in the sense that something apparently undesirable about the product you're advertising could unlock a surprising and persuasive way to sell it – but it equally applies to the startling originality and purpose that may be hiding beneath the surface-level inadequacy of an idea.

Another debilitating symptom of allowing your writing to be ruled by the jury is that you start writing to please the wrong people. We are, of course, required to write what our audience needs to hear – but we are not required to extend this same courtesy to anyone outside of this targeted group – your friends, doubters and bosses included. It's a little like a Joseph Conrad line from Heart of Darkness, where the storyteller is described as 'showing in this remark the weakness of many tellers of tales who seem so often unaware of what their audience would best like to hear'. What we have to remember is that we, the copywriters, know precisely what our audience would best like to hear – and nothing should divert us from that path.

Allowing our jury to persuade us to immediately shred and burn an idea they believe will embarrass us (or rather, them) could easily result in your most beautiful writing shrivelling away before it had the chance to outgrow its ugliness.

Pierre says we must 'dismantle the censors in our head and give yourself a license to write'. They may, and probably will, regenerate as often as you take them apart – the trick is to write like the wind whenever they're in pieces.

Copywriting is

SILLY

(Or, listen to Larkin)

Whenever I find myself taking my job as a copywriter too *seriously*, I read a poem by Philip Larkin called 'Sunny Prestatyn'. Tempted as I am to pad out the word count by reproducing the whole thing here, I shan't.

But I do urge anyone who makes their living in the endearingly preposterous world of creative advertising to copy it out and pin it somewhere near your desk.

In the poem, Larkin describes a billboard ad urging people to visit 'Sunny Prestatyn'. Unceremoniously 'slapped up one day in March' the model on the poster becomes gradually more 'snaggle-toothed and boss-eyed' as local urchins systematically deface the ad until, one day, she finds herself in possession of 'a tuberous cock and balls*'.

(*Shit like this is why I read Larkin.)

At the end of the poem, the torn and tattered poster has served its term on the billboard and is replaced, absurdly, by a 'fight cancer' advert.

For me, the poem is a reminder not only of the brief – and often unhappy – life of creative work, but also how flippantly it's regarded by almost everybody outside of the industry.

Sunny Prestatyn reminds me not only to avoid taking the business of copywriting too seriously, but also that to be a copywriter is to be wilfully silly.

Ours is an odd profession where the business of what we do is often directly at odds with the mechanics of imagination.

Creativity, I believe, requires play. It demands an atmosphere of fearless nonsense – permission to express your oddest observations without hesitation or filtration.

As soon as a copywriter falls into the trap of taking it all too seriously – which we all do, frequently and unavoidably – it breaks contact with that burbling spring of silliness so necessary to our craft.

Writing about Coco Chanel, Karl Lagerfeld (probably not your immediate pick as a champion for larking about) said 'Fashion does not have to prove that it is serious. It is the proof that intelligent frivolity can be something creative and positive'.

Frivolity, in copywriting, is too often treated as an underground activity. It is confined and concealed, and when it comes to sharing ideas, the silliness in which they were conceived is self-consciously tucked out of sight.

Edward Gorey, a demi-god of silliness, apparently once said 'to take my work seriously would be the height of folly'.

And yet I know I've been guilty of wanting to be seen as a serious professional producing serious thoughts. But it is, quite frankly, exhausting to masquerade as a serious person doing a serious job when you are neither.

In fact there is an argument that a copywriter's capacity for silliness is a more accurate and affirming indicator of their ability than the po-ness of their face.

There's another poem (don't be fooled, I only know about four) by Charles Bukowski called '59 Cents a Pound' where he writes:

there's nothing better than the joke
of us
the seriousness of us
the dullness of us.

And that too serves as a warning for copywriters. We have worked hard to shed our seriousness – or rather, to avoid contracting it. We have cultivated an inherent sense of absurdity and frivolity, purely because we need that within us to produce something surprising and strange and new.

Strangling that, solely because you have an inbox and an online calendar and performance reviews with a man in a stripy tie, is a fatal misunderstanding of what you want – and need – to be good at.

Stay silly, I say, or, for your own sanity, stay away from copywriting.

SILLY

Copywriting is

FINISHING

(Or, getting out of your copy while you still can)

Knowing whether or not you have *finished* what you're writing is a little like knowing whether or not you've fallen in love. If you have to think about it too much, you haven't.

But if starting to write can feel like struggling to uncork your imagination, finishing is like forcing that cork back into a frothing bottle neck.

To have dragged and debased ourselves to free the words, it can feel incredibly difficult to stand them down.

Michael Baldwin's advice on finishing a story is 'to get out of it quickly'. Copywriting can be viewed the same way. Finishing what you're writing cannot feel like a drawn out, tearful farewell on a picturesque train platform. It is a leap from a window, possibly without taking the time to open it first.

The only real way to know if you should stop is to stop. Or rather, to pause and review what you've done and ask some rather important questions.

These questions, though, might be best framed in terms of what you've done badly rather than searching for your triumphs.

For example, ask what in the brief you could have missed rather than what you have caught.

Ask if your writing is confusing rather than listing off what is entirely clear about it.

And, rather than asking yourself how enthralling and eloquent your writing is, ask if it is boring. (This is probably the most essential point for, as Nassim Nicholas Taleb points out, 'You may eventually forgive and befriend someone who harmed you. Never someone who bored you.')

By looking, objectively not anxiously, for the faults you get a clear picture of what your copy still needs - which is far more useful for finishing than understanding what it does well.

Another trick to being a more clinical finisher of copywriting starts way before you approach the end. By writing with care, rigour and, above all, discipline you are more likely to arrive at a piece of copy that will stand up well to your final interrogation.

The alternative to this is what Scott Meredith, in Writing to Sell, calls 'first-draftitis - the habit of writing loosely and carelessly because you know you can fix everything in subsequent drafts.'

If you are able to write as if this is your only chance, it will be easier to make a clean getaway. If you write sloppily, telling yourself that you'll do it better next time, then getting out of your copy will be like freeing yourself from a maniac's basement. Painful, frightening and possibly fatal. (There is, as you may have realised, a fine – but not un-crossable – line between writing with care and writing with dynamite. Copywriting is defusal *and* it is detonation, the trick is knowing which one the occasion demands.)

The most satisfying and effective way to step out of your copy is through a line that feels beautifully final. As if writing anything beyond this point would feel, at best, unnecessary and, at worst, destructive. I realise, writing this, that I have now teed myself up to produce such a confident and conclusive ending line.

Instead, like a coward, I shall share my favourite ending line from the world of literature - a place where you will find the very best, and the very worst, ways to end a story.

Mine is from James Salter's Light Years, a novel so complex and beautiful that, if you or I thought too hard about giving it the ending it deserved we'd need a tractor to haul around our first, unfinished, draft.

Instead, with the confidence of someone who knows how to make a full stop that people cannot forget, Salter ends his book with this:

'Yes, he thought, I am ready, I have always been ready, I am ready at last'.

And who'd be stupid enough to ruin an ending like that?

FINISHING.

CAN YOU TEACH CREATIVITY?

(Or, the final thought)

Short answer:
yes.

Why not? Creativity is too intangible, too indecipherable a quality to subscribe to the same genetic predispositions as, say, how high you can jump or how slowly your muscles tire. And anyway, in the case of those two examples, you will struggle to find a sports psychologist who ascribes the likelihood of your success so heavily to the numbers on your genetic lottery ticket.

The answer lies somewhere in the understanding of what we mean by 'creativity'. It's a human attribute that existed long before the first painting was daubed, or the first novel printed – chiefly because, without it, prehistoric man would not have had the imagination required to make the tools, light the fires or hunt the dinosaurs (yes, I know) they needed for the species to survive.

We are, of course, talking about a creativity that is not a prerequisite for survival but one that comes about by choice, not necessity.

Nevertheless, the human brain remains so fascinating and mysterious purely because of its capacity for evolution and adaptation.

Also, the concept of a 'creative person' has, like any reductive identity, become such a prevalent stereotype that when we think of who, and who is not, capable of creative thought it becomes more about appearances than application. Look at that person in the neon dungarees, unicycling their way to the Avocado Café, that human is, without question, 'a creative'.

The teachability of creativity is so impossible to chart that the conversation descends into a matter of opinions and experience. I see students who, at first glance, you would assign to a million other vocations other than creativity, and yet, crucially, they have made the decision that this is a part of themselves they wish to unlock.

It may seem trivial to say that a creative future is dependent only on how much you want it, just like saying if I (a schoolboy footballer whose first touch was once described as 'nauseating') practiced keepy-ups for an uninterrupted 10,000 hours, could be playing for Blackburn Rovers. (Dream big, kids.)
But my experience (which in this case, like everybody else, can be my only reasonable

basis for an opinion) is that creativity infects the mind like a virus. The more you see of what it can do, the more you want to stretch and break and harness it yourself.

If anything, equipping a young mind with the creative instinct is not even the hardest part of the job. Getting them to focus that creativity, to cross-breed their imagination with a sense of discipline, is far more challenging than getting a young person to see the world in a new way.

I sometimes worry that the doubts around teaching creativity are built around a reflexive, defensive nostalgia. It's surprising how many people who have achieved the greatest creative success will go to remarkable lengths to reassure us that what they achieved was in-spite of, rather than owing to, what they were taught. This is an understandable argument when we're talking about wonderful creatives who failed their Biology GCSE. But how many of those great achievers would, as their younger selves, have been so scornful about an opportunity to refine and develop their creative foundations?

Another prominent complaint is that any individual or institution that teaches creativity is actually in the business of indoctrination – breeding class after class of homologous, by-the-textbook creatives who are just as terrified of the unexpected as a trainee mortgage broker.

This is such monumental bullshit, I dread to think of the wreckage that would have been inflicted to the bull-anus that even attempted to deposit such a notion.

There is no formula for teaching creativity in the same way there is no formula in professional, commercial creativity. If there was, this entire industry would have evaporated like tramp vomit in July.

No one who teaches creativity would ever claim they produce masterpiece creatives. No one, and correct me if I'm wrong, in the history of any creative endeavour could ever claim to be the finished article. What we do produce are young people with belief in their own imaginative ability, a sense of capability that makes them ready to enter the industry with a voice – rather than skulk quietly in and hope no one laughs at their ideas on the first day.

Equally, no one who teaches creativity does so with the belief that the lessons they administer constitute all the learning any creative will ever need. We learn til we die, or we have not been living right.

There is no 'correct' way to discover your creative potential, in the same way there is no 'correct' way to react to a seagull stealing your ice lolly. But, if there is no right way, who can say what creative teachers are doing is so very wrong?

About the author

Andrew Boulton is a copywriter and lecturer in creative advertising. He has written for brands and agencies across the UK and far beyond (some very big ones, plenty of tiny ones) and writes a copywriting column for The Drum. He can grow a beard, but it's not great.

From the same *publisher*...

"I love this book. Anything I spend my time on, I either have to learn something or be entertained, with this book I get both - along with great art direction. The only problem is that the people it takes the piss out of won't know how funny it is. But that's okay, they'll buy it thinking it's a genuine 'How to' guide."

– Dave Trott, Author and Advertising Legend.

ISOLATED
Talks®

"This is without doubt, one of the most valuable and vital platforms for sharing ideas out there and the Samaritans save countless lives."

– Nick Ellis, Founder of Halo.

"A minefield of pure gold. Such a refreshingly brilliant podcast, none of the usual regurgitated nonsense you hear at marketing events and conferences. This is genuine, interesting, jargon-free and brilliant. The standard of guests is incredible, superb witty host. Pure gold."

– Apple Podcast Review.